LEARNING TOGETHER

CEM NON-VERBAL REASONING
PRACTICE TEST 1

ADVICE AND INSTRUCTIONS ON COMPLETING THIS TEST

(THIS PRACTICE TEST MUST BE COMPLETED IN THE STANDARD FORMAT WAY)

1. There are 75 questions in this test.

2. Start at question 1 and work your way to question 75.

3. If you are unable to complete a question leave it and go to the next one.

4. Do not think about the question you have just left as this wastes time.

5. If you change an answer make sure the change is clear.

6. If there is time left, review your answers and go back and answer any questions that you missed.

7. You may do any rough work on the test paper or on another piece of paper.

8. This test provides practice in the various question types that your child may meet and therefore no time limit has been set.

9. This test reflects the type of non-verbal reasoning questions set by CEM but we cannot guarantee that the 11+ exam your child takes will have the same layout or content as this practice test.

10. An adult may be able to explain any questions you do not understand.

Published by Learning Together 11+ Publishers Ltd, 18 Shandon Park, Belfast, BT5 6NW. Phone/fax 028 90402086
e-mail: online@learningtogether.co.uk. Website:- www.learningtogether.co.uk Online Platform:- www.onlineelevenplusexams.co.uk

All rights reserved. No part of this publication, in whole or in part, may be reproduced, stored in a retrieval system or transmitted, in any form, or by any means, electronic, mechanical, photycoping, recording or otherwise, without the prior written consent of the copyright owner.

Whilst the content of this test is believed to be true and accurate at the time of going to press, neither the authors nor publishers can accept any legal responsibility or liability for any errors or omissions that may have been made.
THE COPYRIGHT OF THIS TEST WILL BE FORCEFULLY DEFENDED IN COURT.

Which shape is the same but facing the opposite direction?
Circle one letter each time. Look at this example.

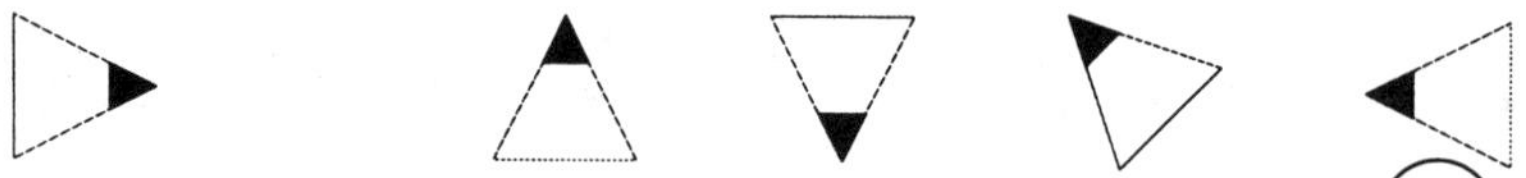

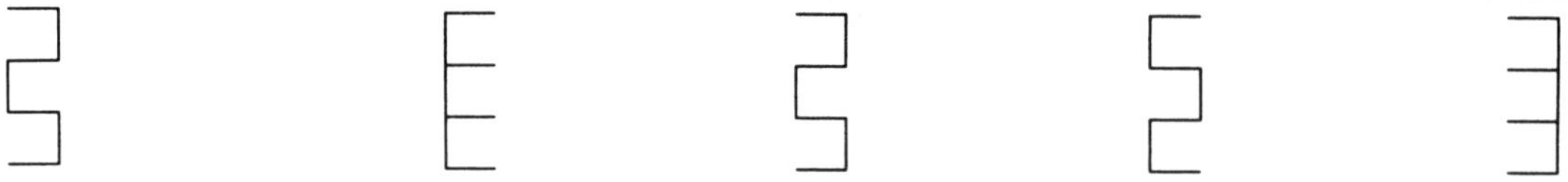

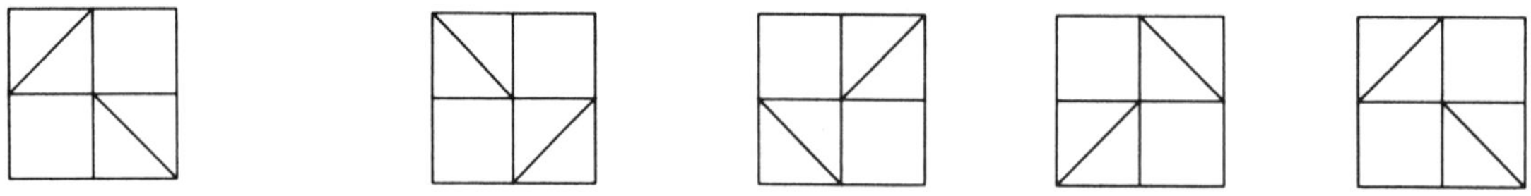

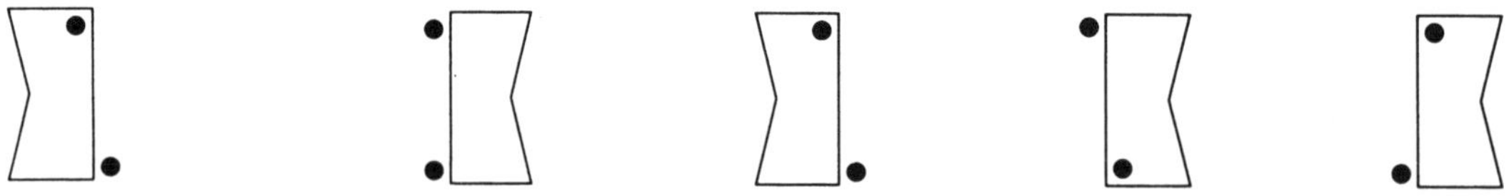

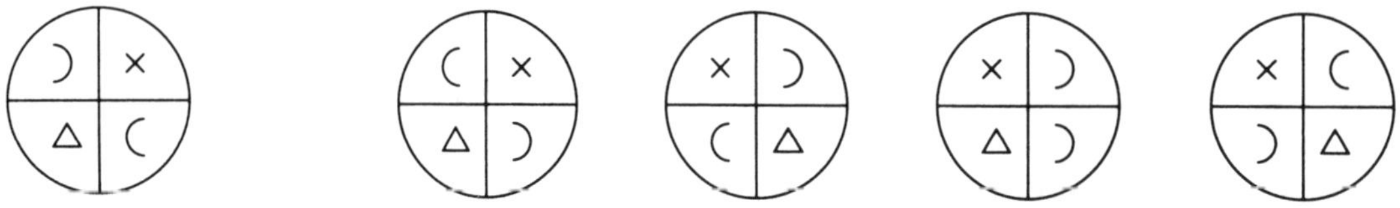

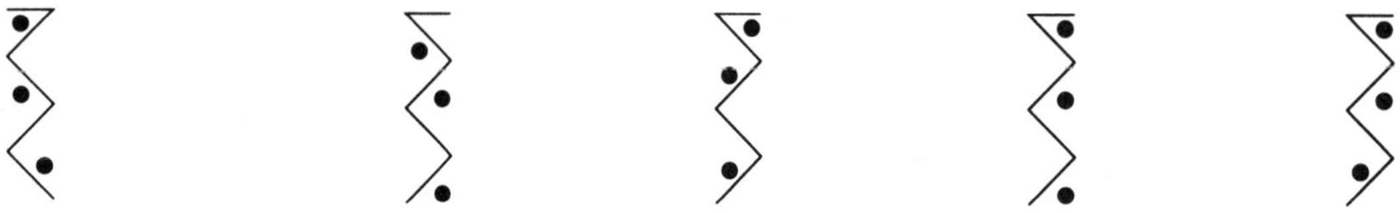

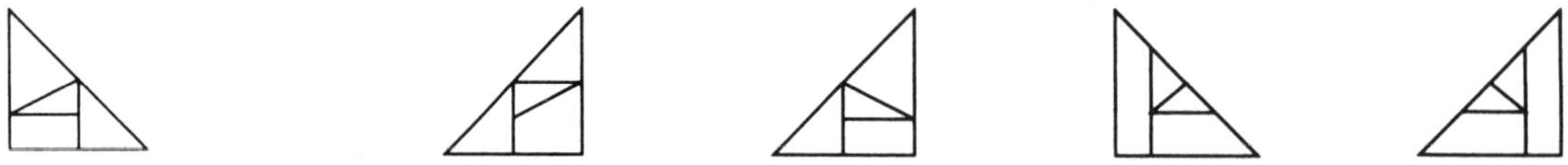

1.
2.
3.
4.
5.
6.
7.
8.

Test One Page 2

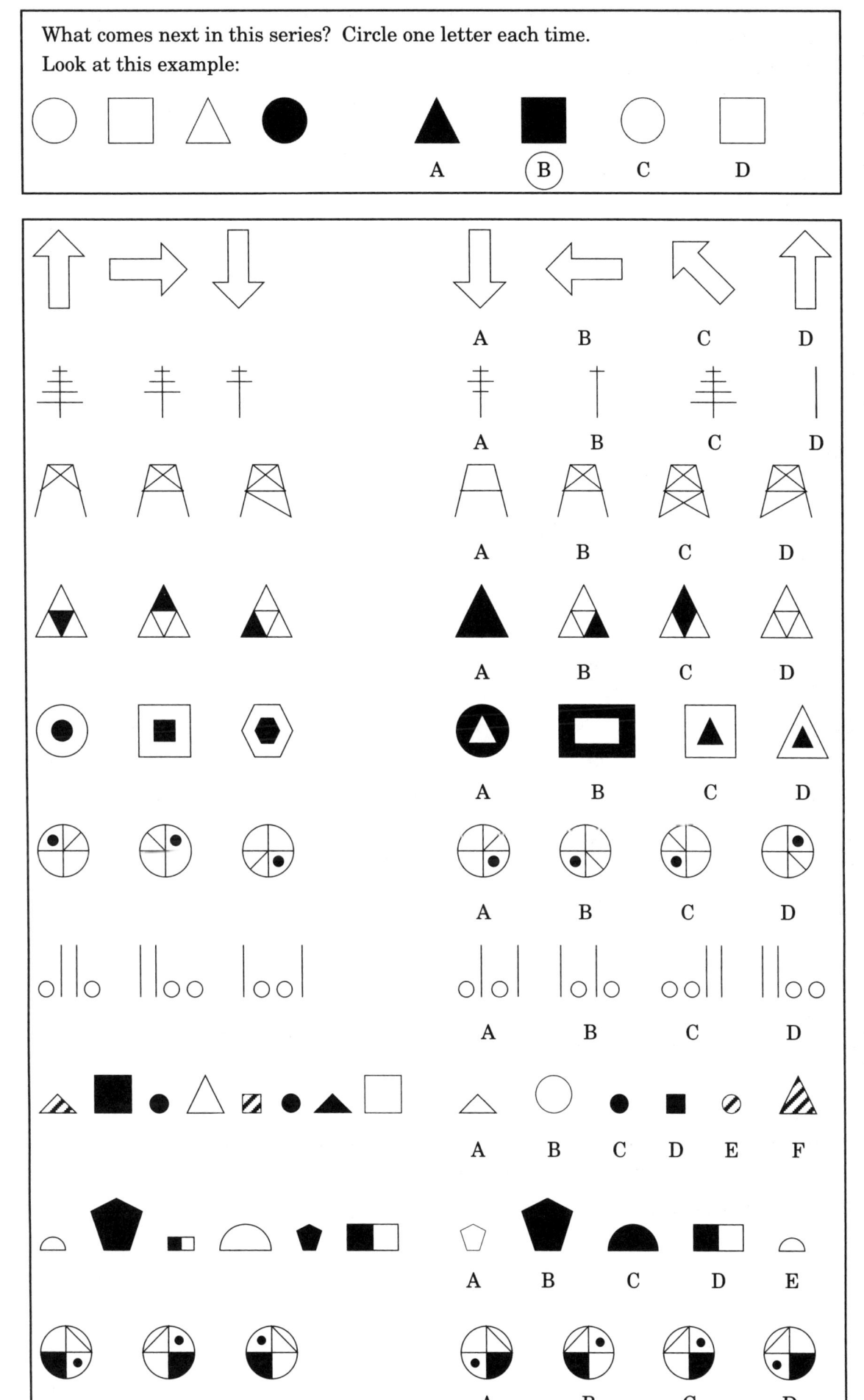

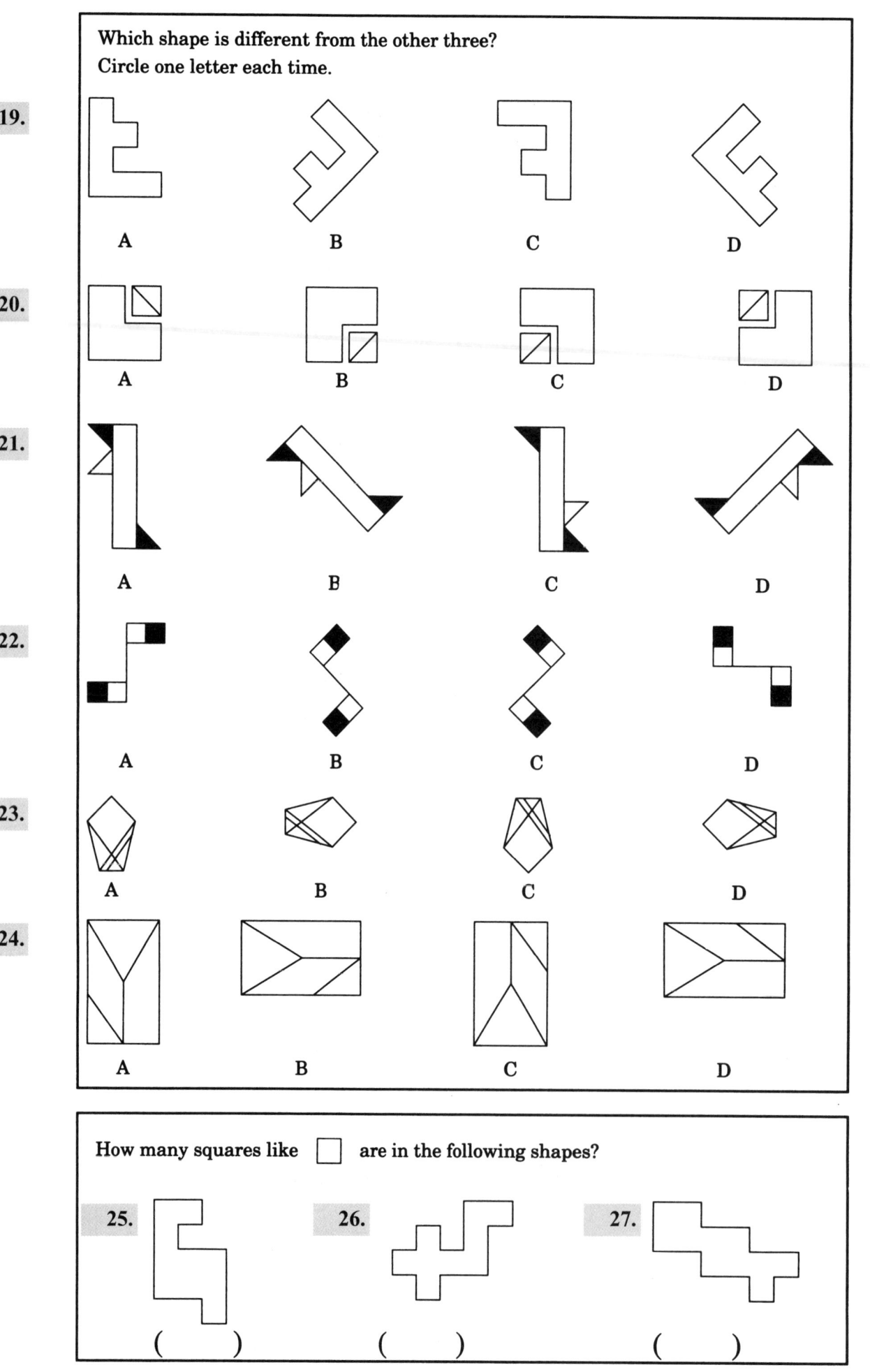

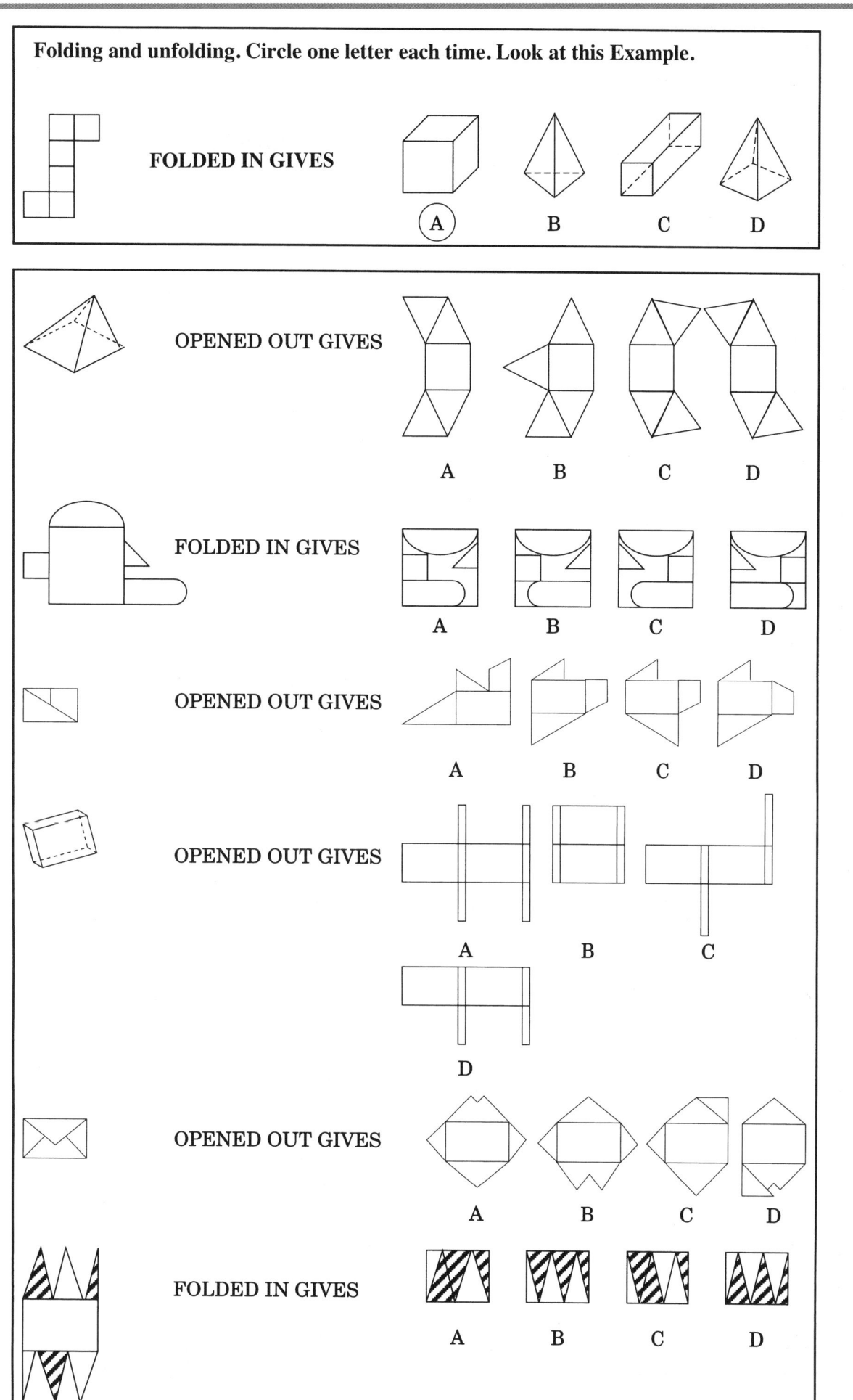

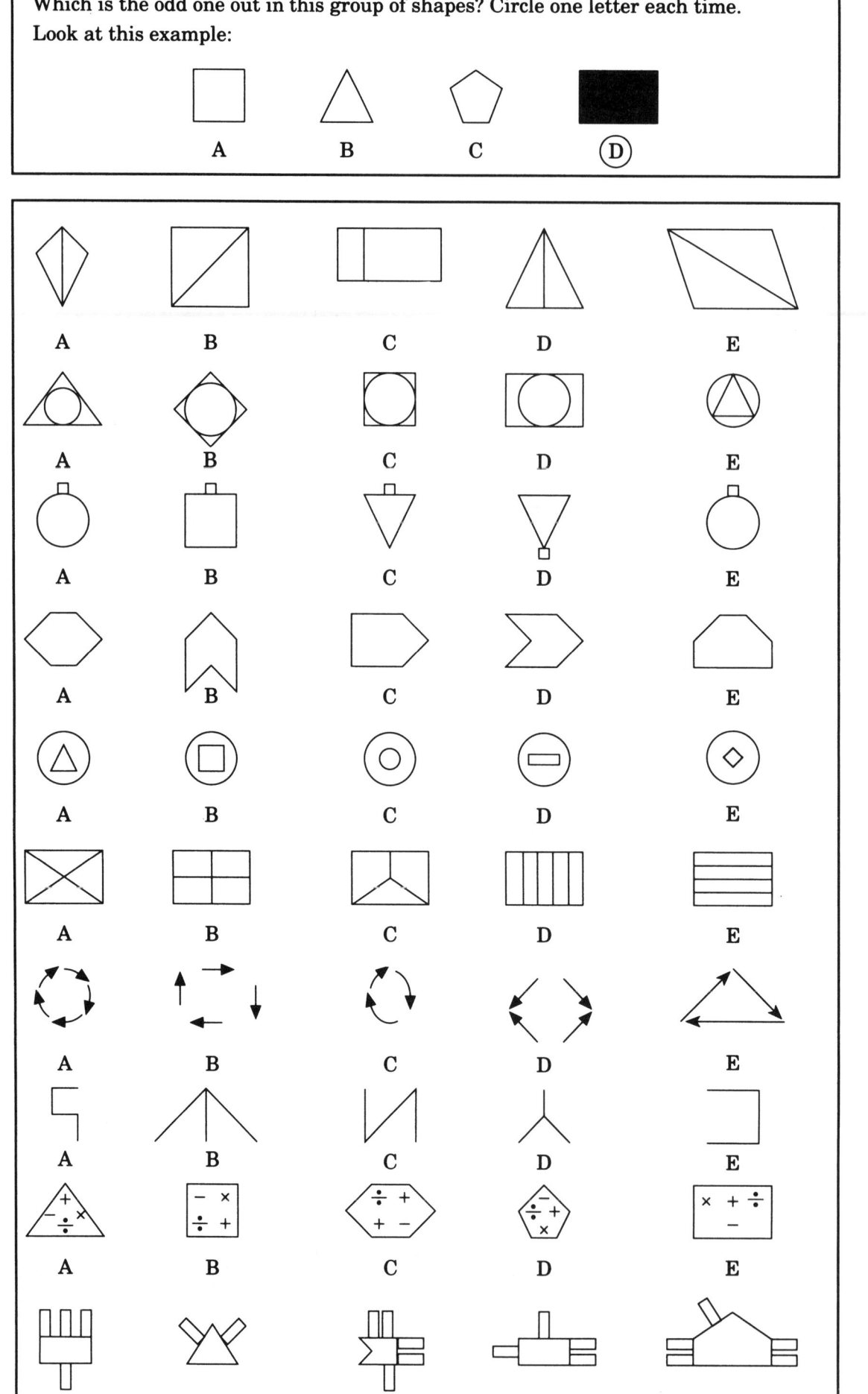

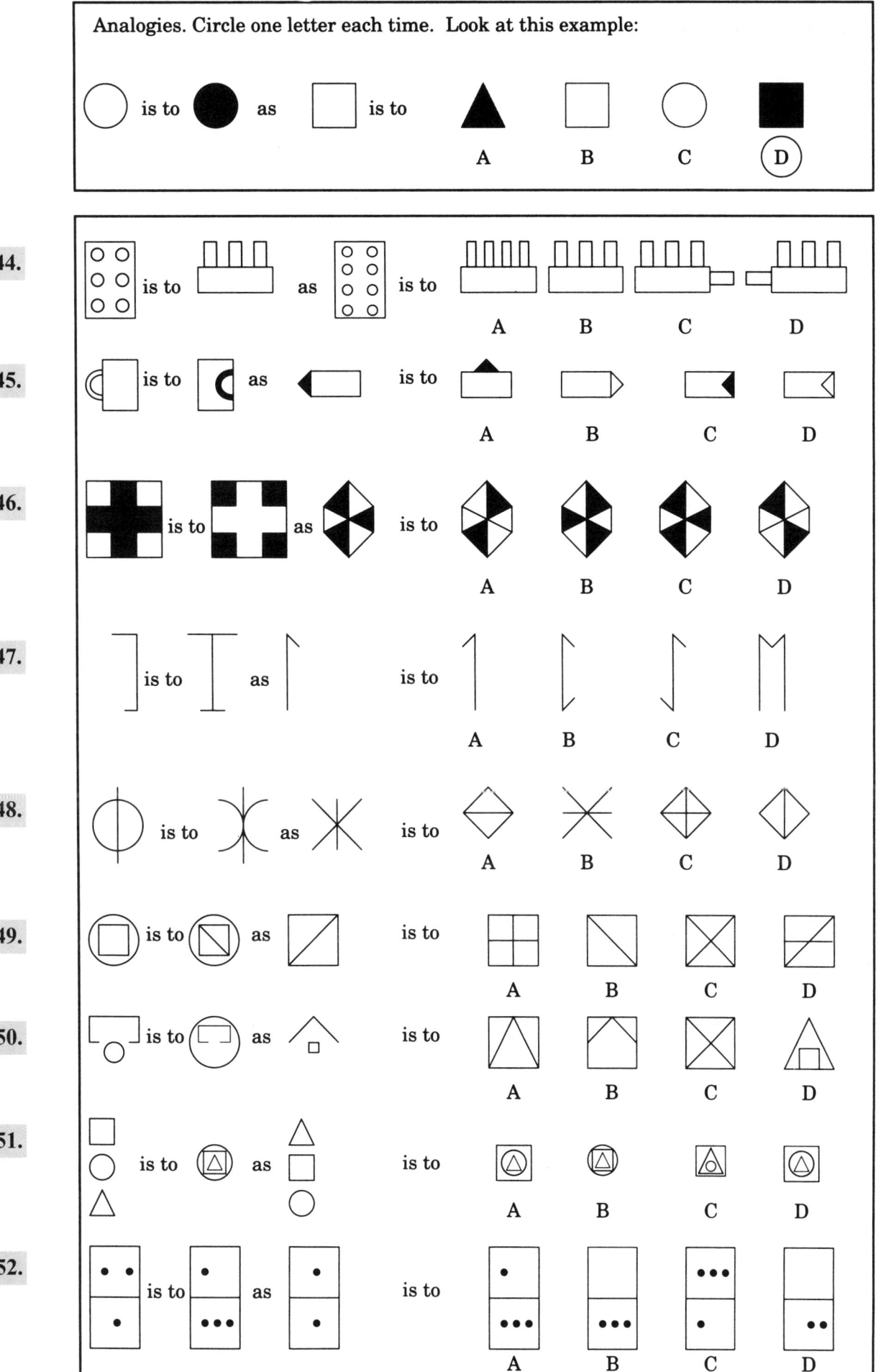

Which two are exactly the same? Circle two letters each time.

53.

54.

55.

56.

57.

58.

In these questions the two shapes are either added together or subtracted from each other. The shapes do not turn. Circle one answer. Look at this example.

59.
60.
61.
62.
63.
64.
65.
66.
67.
68.

Which shape does not have a horizontal or a verticle line of symmetry? Circle one letter each time.

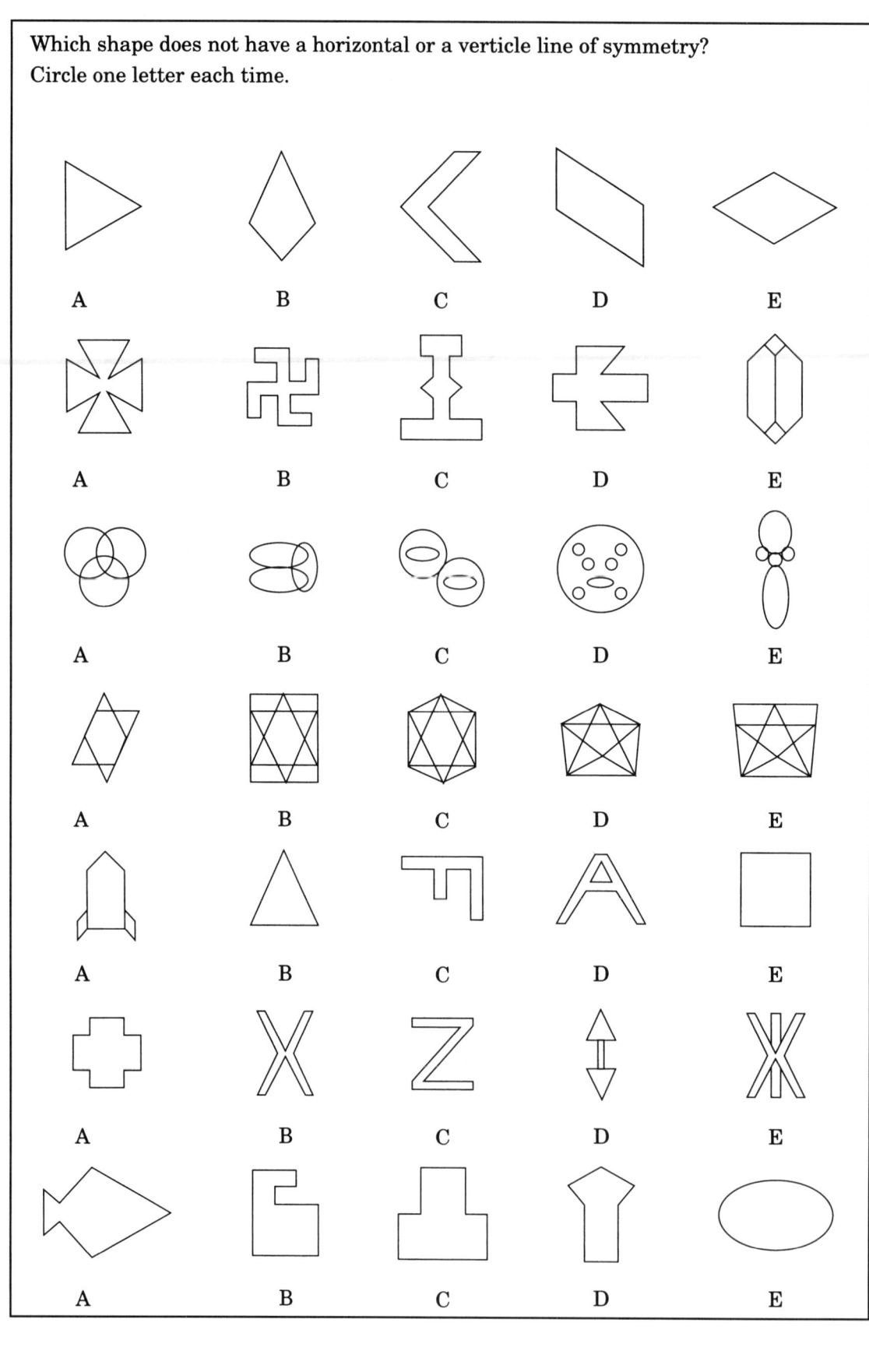

Answers to CEM Non-Verbal Reasoning Practice Test 1.

Question type			Question type		
Reflection	1	C	Odd One Out	39	C
	2	C		40	D
	3	C		41	A
	4	D		42	C
	5	D		43	B
	6	D	Analogies	44	A
	7	B		45	D
	8	C		46	B
Series	9	B		47	D
	10	B		48	D
	11	C		49	C
	12	B		50	B
	13	D		51	C
	14	B		52	B
	15	C	Two the Same	53	C & E
	16	E		54	A & E
	17	E		55	A & E
	18	D		56	C & E
Shape Differerent from Other	19	D		57	C & D
	20	C		58	B & E
	21	D	Two Added or Subtracted Shapes	59	C
	22	C		60	B
	23	C		61	D
	24	D		62	A
How Many Squares	25	10		63	B
	26	9		64	C
	27	11		65	D
Folding an Unfolding	28	D		66	C
	29	B		67	D
	30	B		68	B
	31	C	Symmetry	69	D
	32	B		70	B
	33	C		71	C
Odd One Out	34	C		72	A
	35	E		73	C
	36	D		74	C
	37	C		75	B
	38	C			

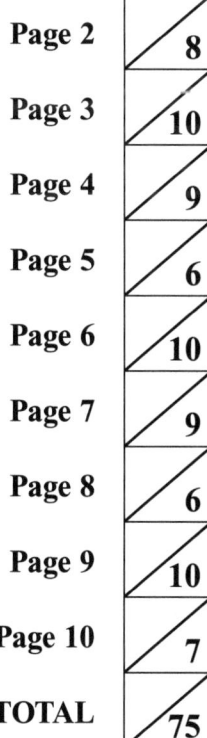

Page 2	8
Page 3	10
Page 4	9
Page 5	6
Page 6	10
Page 7	9
Page 8	6
Page 9	10
Page 10	7
TOTAL	75

Web: - www.Learningtogether.co.uk

Online 11+ platform: - www.onlineelevenplusexams.co.uk

LEARNING TOGETHER

CEM NON-VERBAL REASONING
PRACTICE TEST 2

ADVICE AND INSTRUCTIONS ON COMPLETING THIS TEST

(THIS PRACTICE TEST MUST BE COMPLETED IN THE STANDARD FORMAT WAY)

1. There are 75 questions in this test.

2. Start at question 1 and work your way to question 75.

3. If you are unable to complete a question leave it and go to the next one.

4. Do not think about the question you have just left as this wastes time.

5. If you change an answer make sure the change is clear.

6. If there is time left, review your answers and go back and answer any questions that you missed.

7. You may do any rough work on the test paper or on another piece of paper.

8. This test provides practice in the various question types that your child may meet and therefore no time limit has been set.

9. This test reflects the type of non-verbal reasoning questions set by CEM but we cannot guarantee that the 11+ exam your child takes will have the same layout or content as this practice test.

10. An adult may be able to explain any questions you do not understand.

Published by Learning Together 11+ Publishers Ltd, 18 Shandon Park, Belfast, BT5 6NW. Phone/fax 028 90402086
e-mail: online@learningtogether.co.uk. Website:- www.learningtogether.co.uk Online Platform:- www.onlineelevenplusexams.co.uk
All rights reserved. No part of this publication, in whole or in part, may be reproduced, stored in a retrieval system or transmitted, in any form, or by any means, electronic, mechanical, photycoping, recording or otherwise, without the prior written consent of the copyright owner.
Whilst the content of this test is believed to be true and accurate at the time of going to press, neither the authors nor publishers can accept any legal responsibility or liability for any errors or omissions that may have been made.
THE COPYRIGHT OF THIS TEST WILL BE FORCEFULLY DEFENDED IN COURT.

Look at the shape on the left. Which shadow matches the shape on the left exactly? Circle one letter each time.

A Ⓑ C D

1. A B C D
2. A B C D
3. A B C D
4. A B C D
5. A B C D
6. A B C D
7. A B C D
8. A B C D

What comes next in this series? Circle one letter each time.
Look at this example.

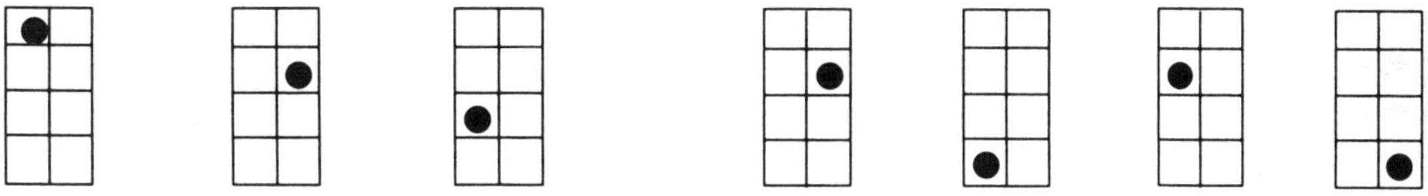

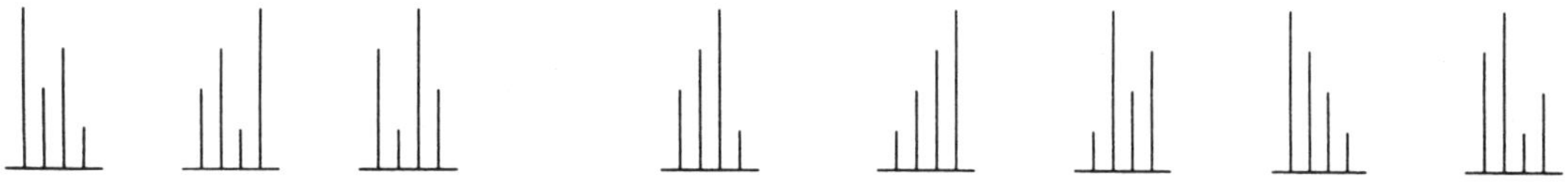

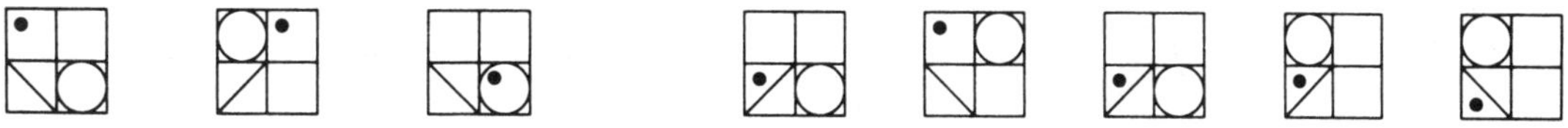

9.
10.
11.
12.
13.
14.
15.
16.

Test Two Page 3

One of the **smaller shapes** will complete the grid.
Decide which is the **correct small shape.** Circle the correct letter.

17. 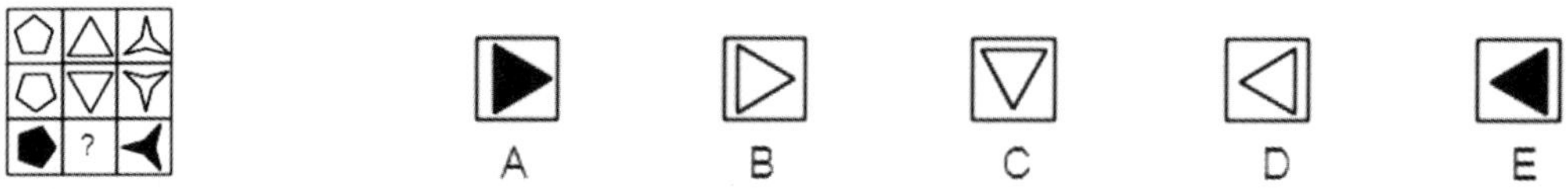
18. 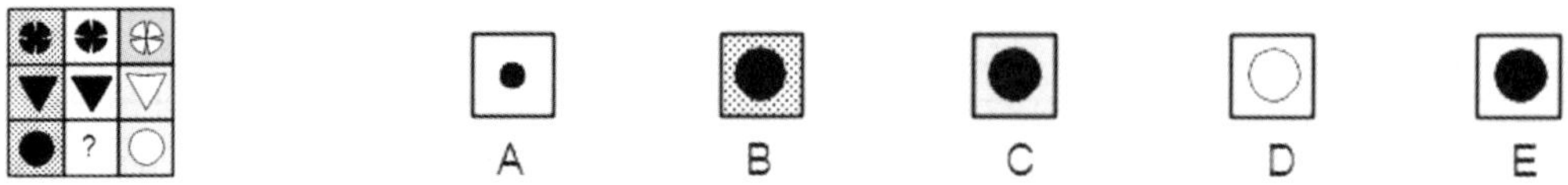
19. 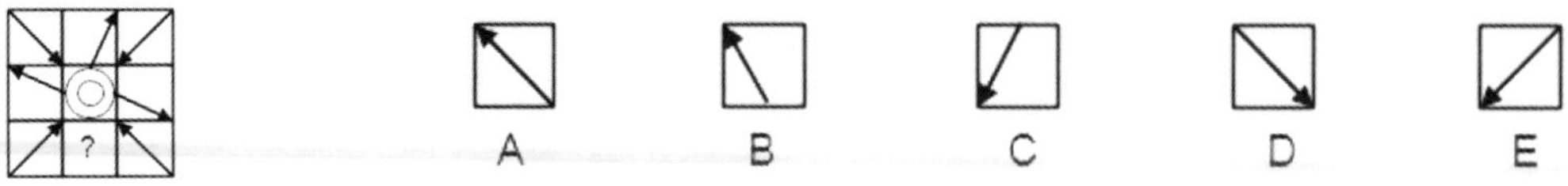
20. 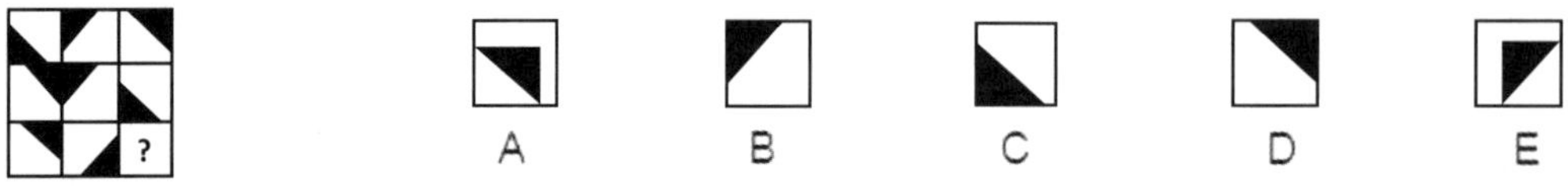
21. 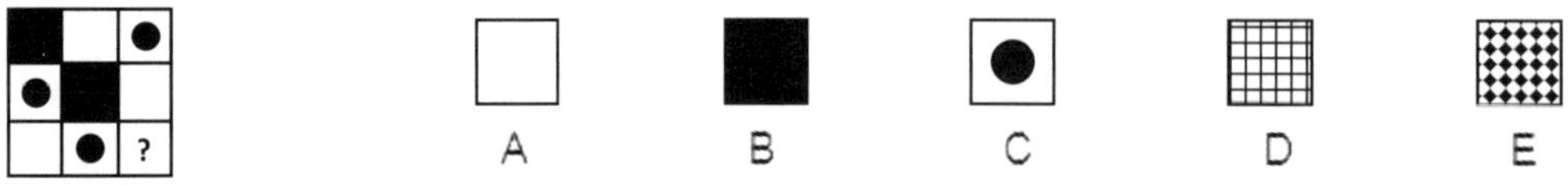
22.

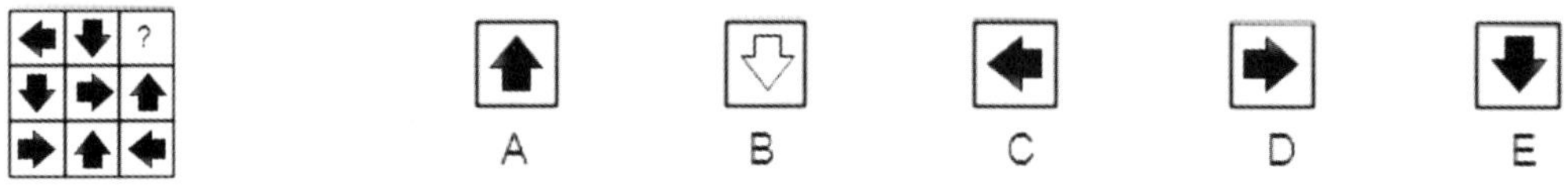

Which larger shape is the small shape hidden in? Circle one letter each time. Look at this example.

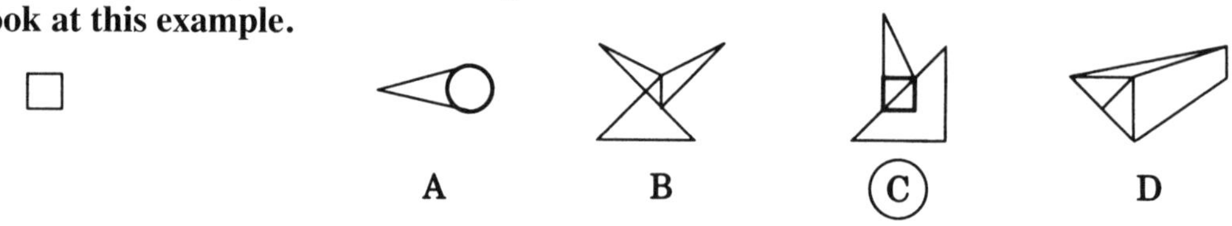

23. 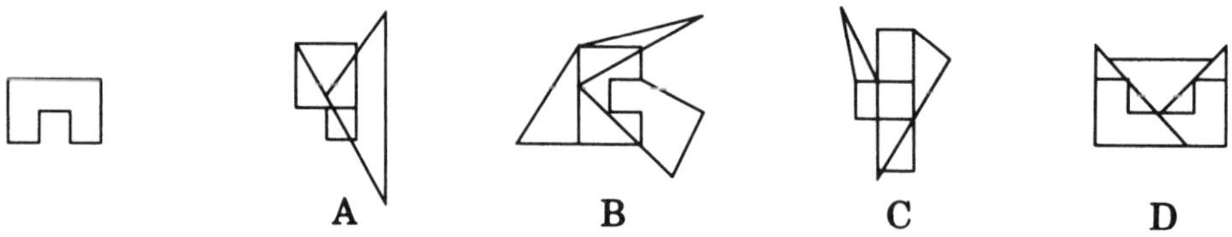
24. 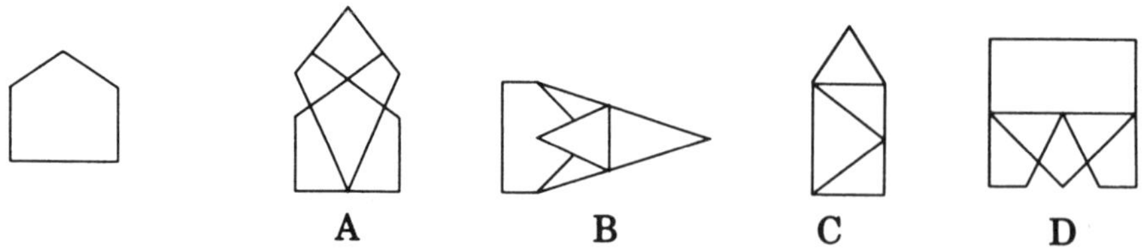
25. 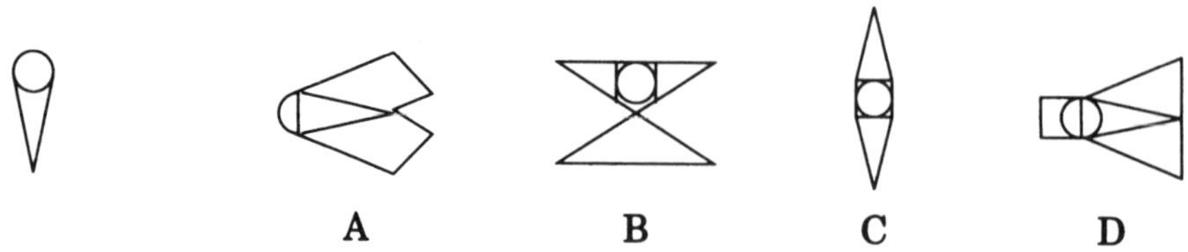
26.

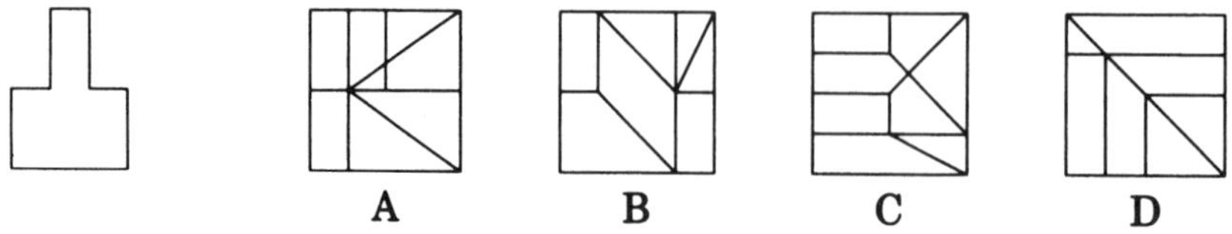

Test Two Page 4

In these questions the two shapes are either added together or subtracted from each other. The shapes do not turn. Circle one answer. Look at this example:

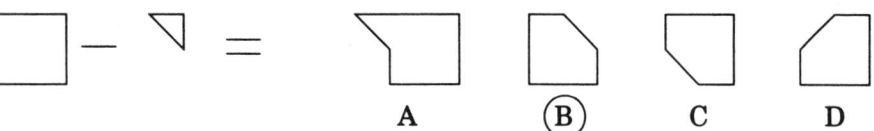

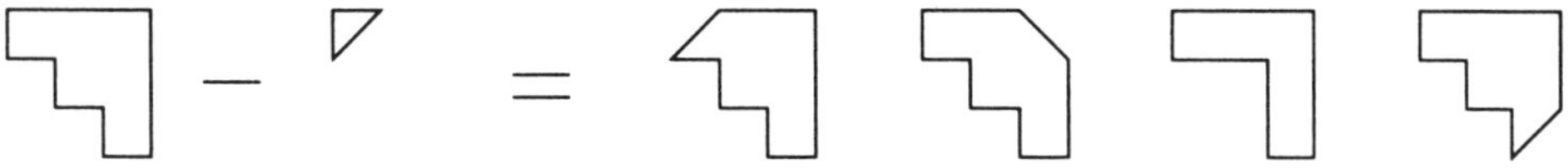

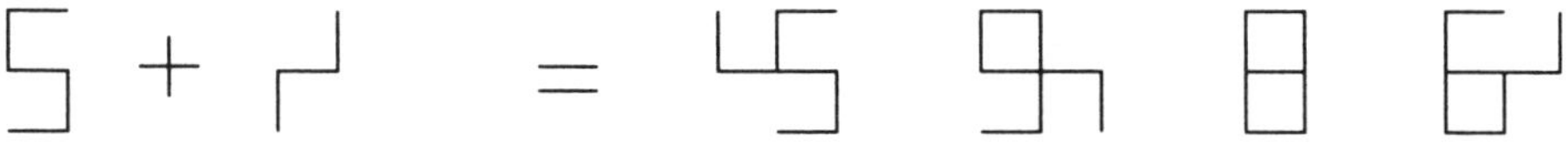

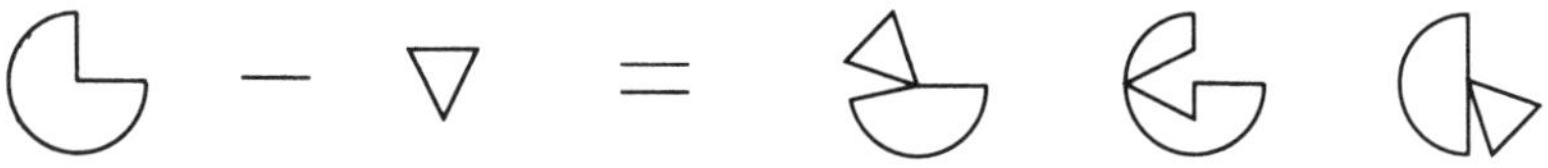

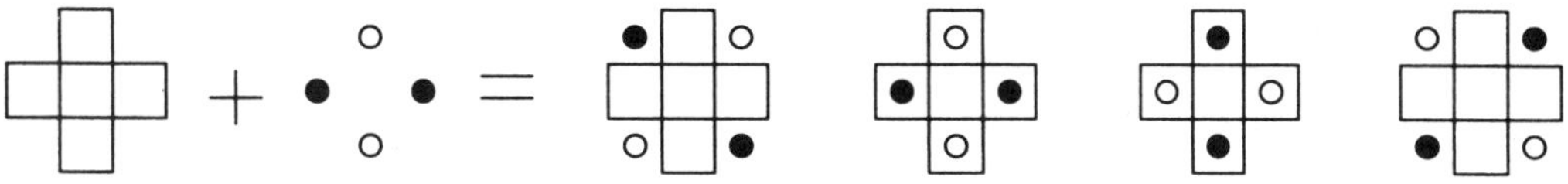

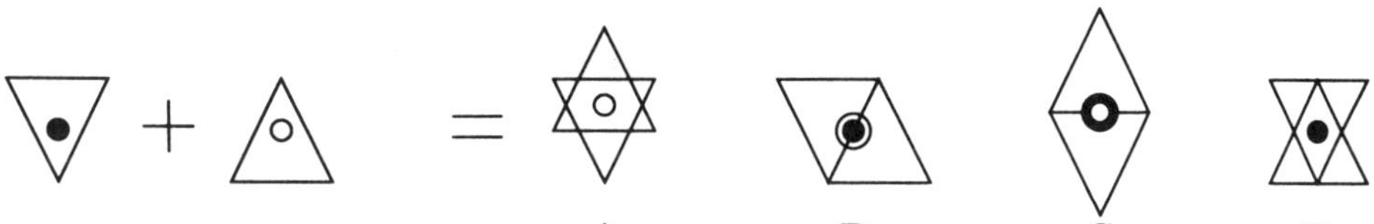

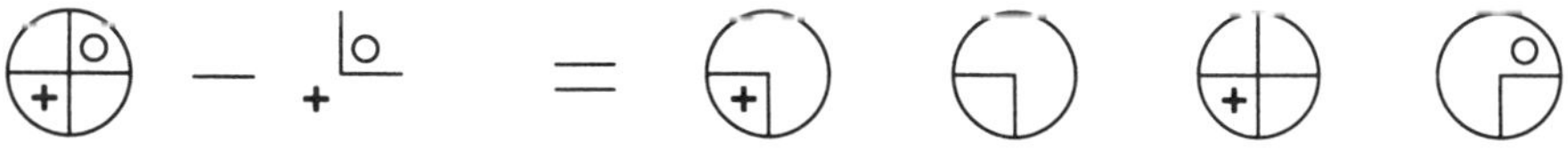

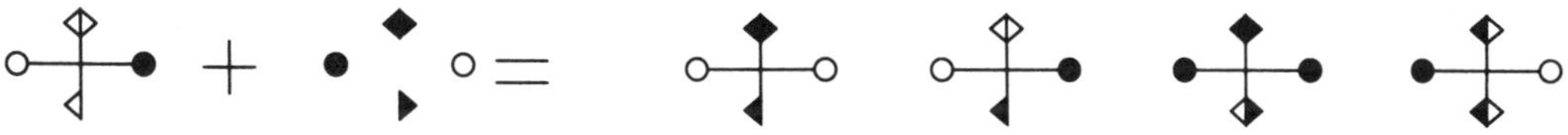

A (B) C D

27.

A B C D

28.

A B C D

29.

A B C D

30.

A B C D

31.

A B C D

32.

A B C D

33.

A B C D

The Nett on the left will fold to form one of the cuboids on the right.
Decide which and circle the correct letter.

34.

A B C D E

35.

A B C D E

36.

A B C D E

10

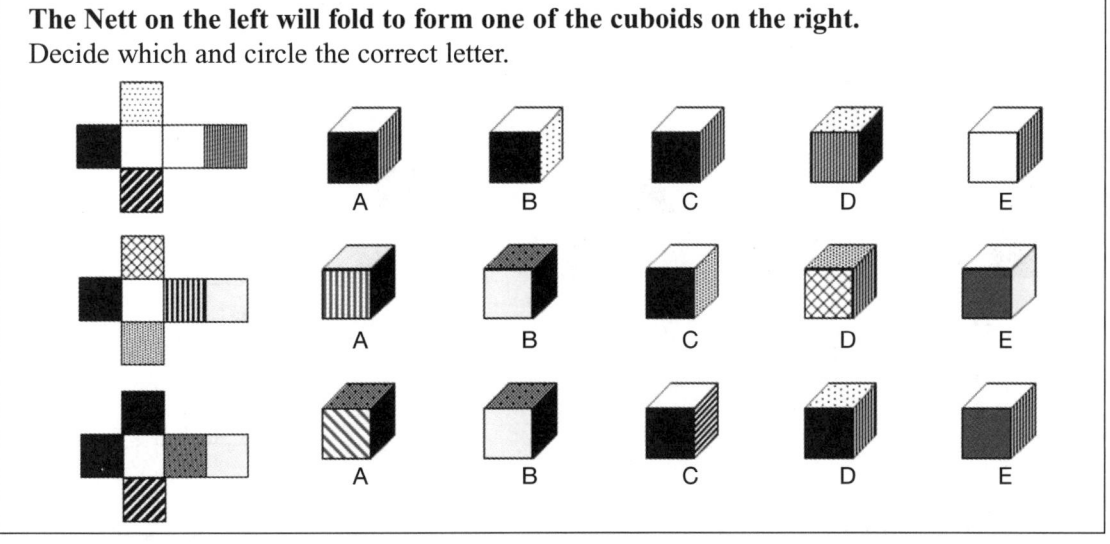

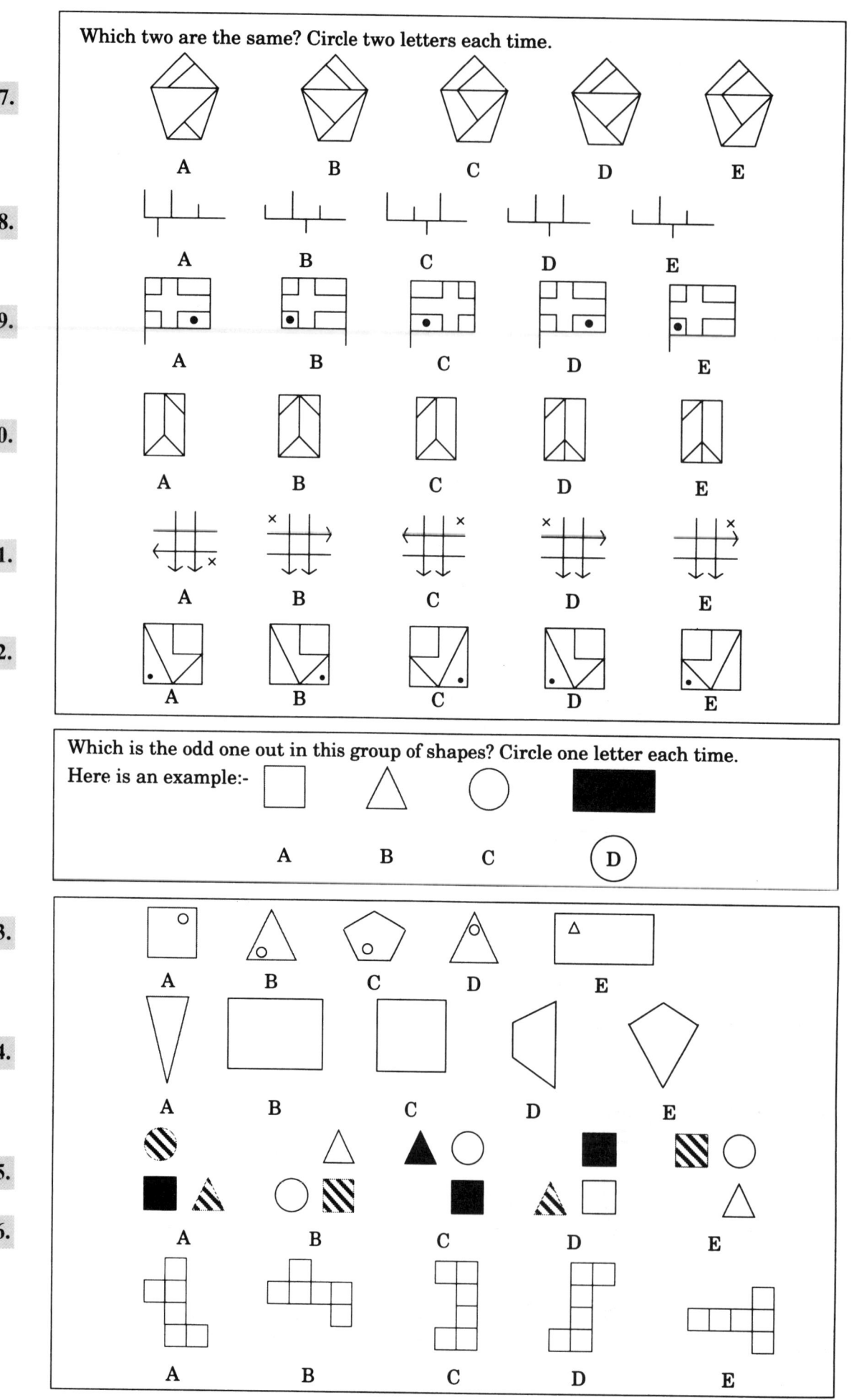

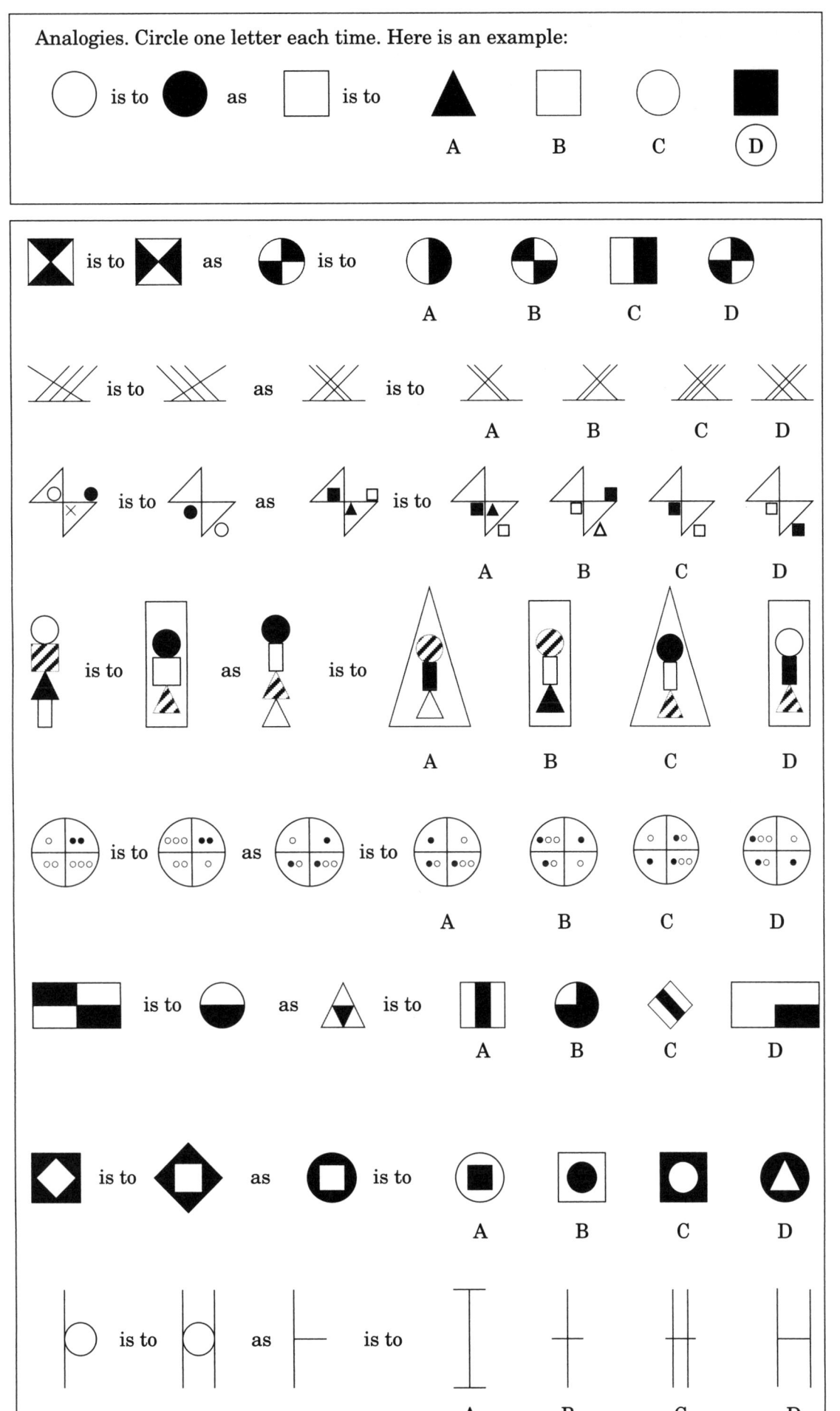

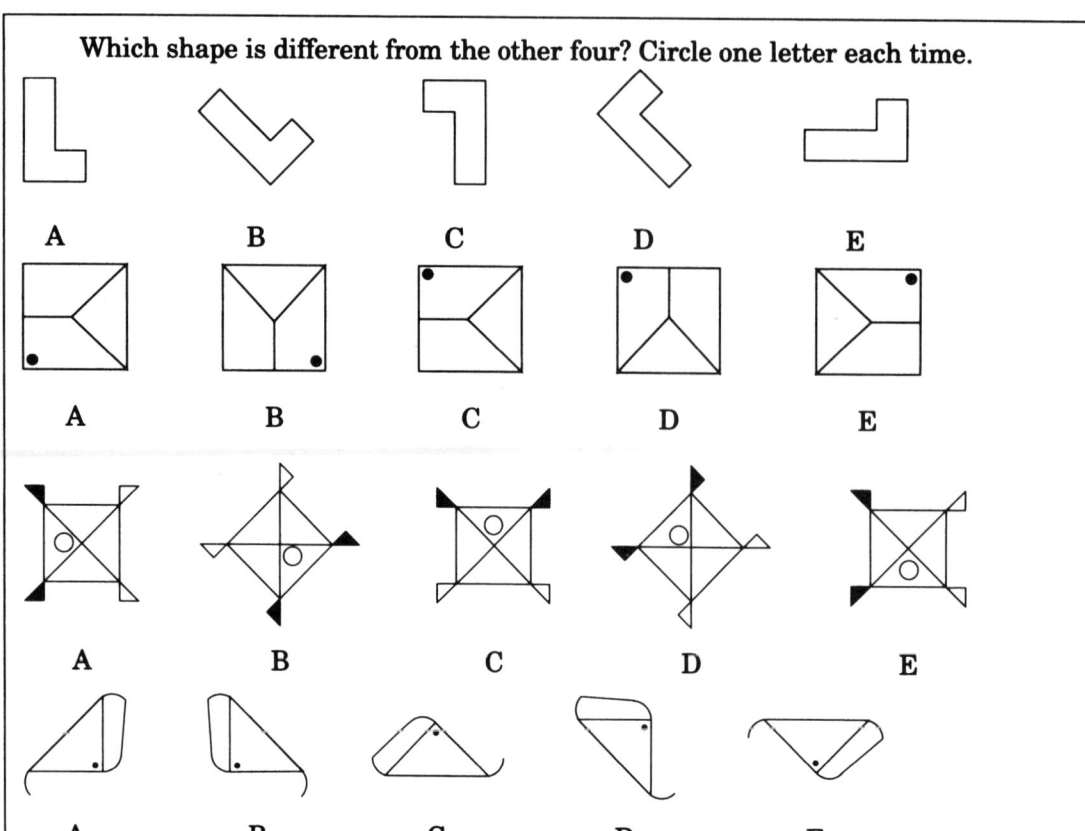

Looking from point X what will you see? Circle one letter each time.

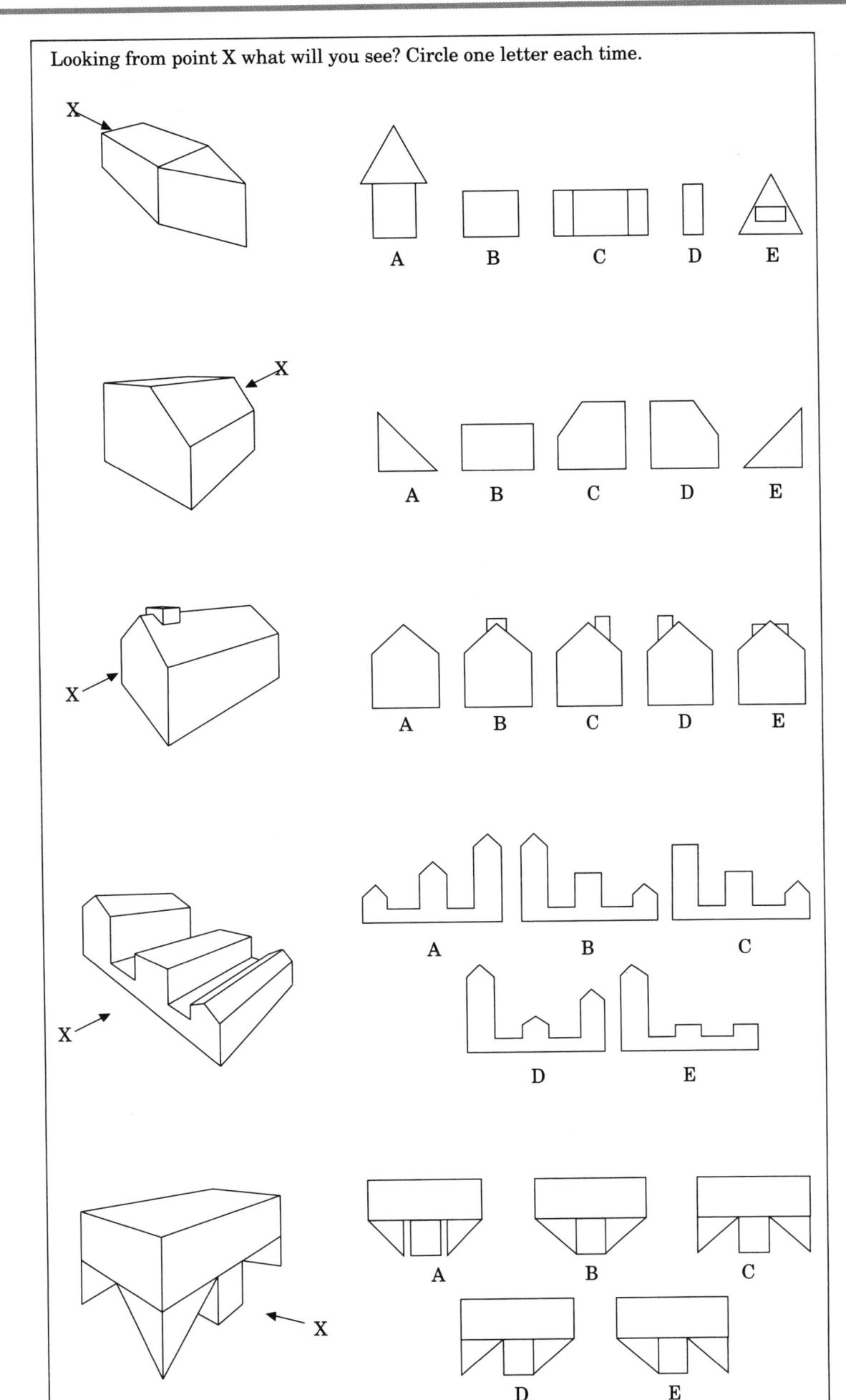

Without turning the pieces over choose which piece completes the white jig-saw. Circle one letter each time.

64.   A   B   C   D

65.   A   B   C   D

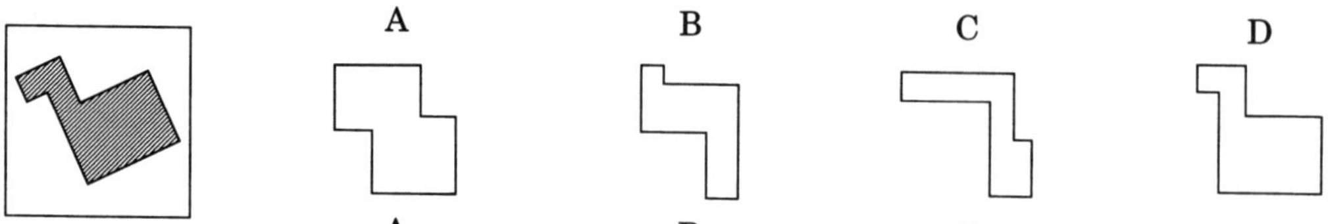

66.   A   B   C   D

67.   A   B   C   D

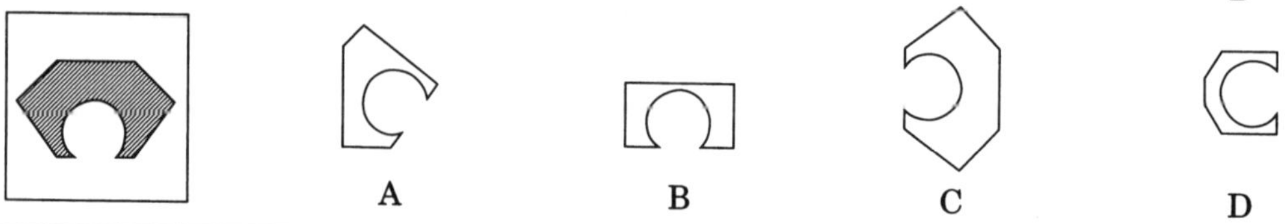

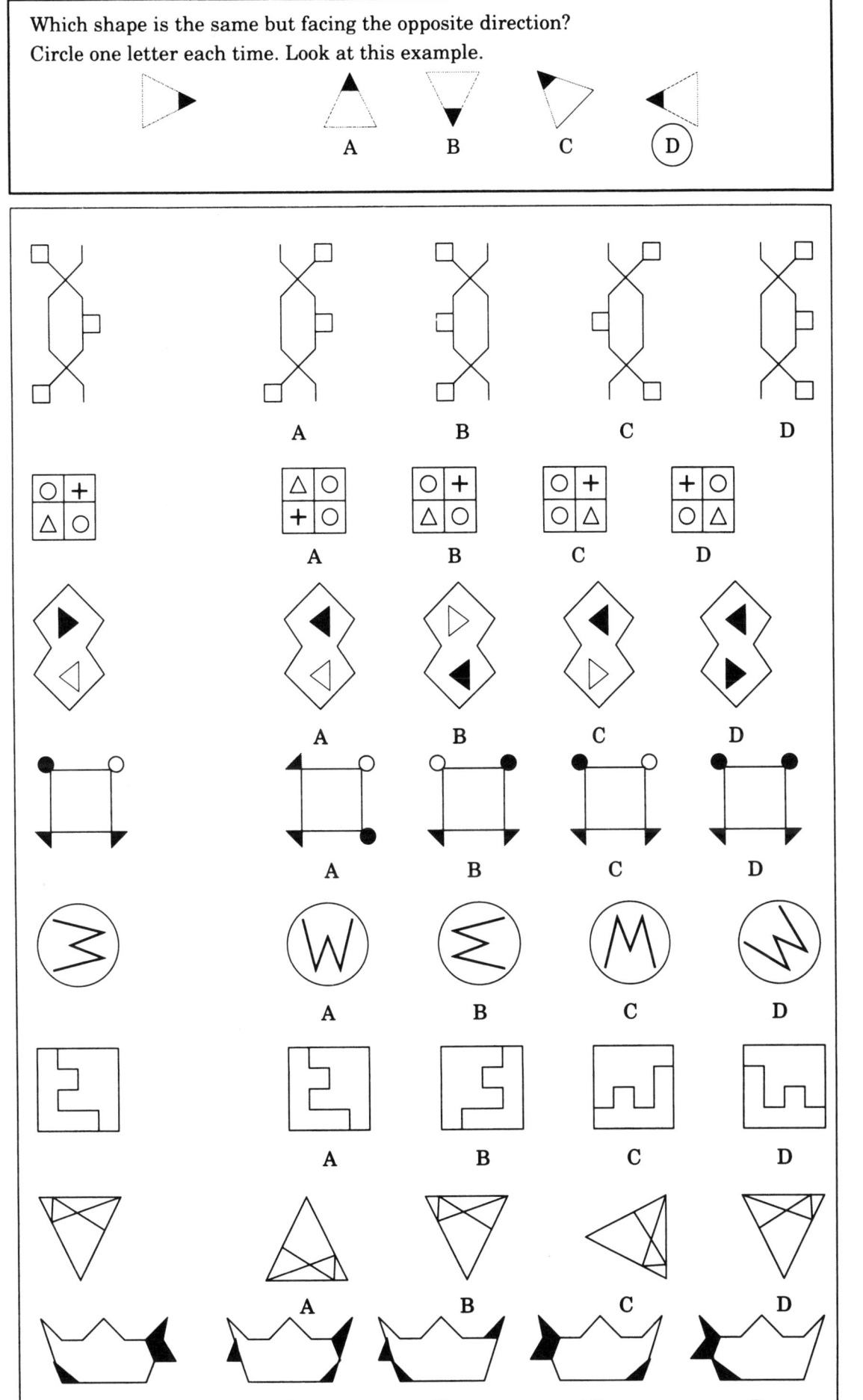

Answers to CEM Non-Verbal Reasoning Practice Test 2.

Question type					
Shadows	1	C	Two the Same	39	A and D
	2	B		40	D and E
	3	D		41	B and D
	4	C		42	A and D
	5	D	Odd One Out	43	E
	6	C		44	A
	7	B		45	D
	8	B		46	C
Series	9	B	Analogies	47	B
	10	D		48	D
	11	D		49	D
	12	C		50	A
	13	C		51	B
	14	C		52	D
	15	B		53	C
	16	D		54	D
Complete Nine Squares	17	A	Different from the Other Four	55	D
	18	E		56	C
	19	C		57	E
	20	C		58	B
	21	B	Viewing 3D Shapes	59	B
	22	D		60	C
Hidden Shape	23	B		61	B
	24	A		62	B
	25	D		63	C
	26	C	Jigsaws	64	B
Adding and Substracting Shapes	27	A		65	D
	28	C		66	B
	29	D		67	C
	30	B	Relections	68	C
	31	D		69	D
	32	B		70	C
	33	C		71	B
Nets to Cuboids	34	D		72	B
	35	B		73	B
	36	C		74	D
Two the Same	37	C and E		75	C
	38	B and E			

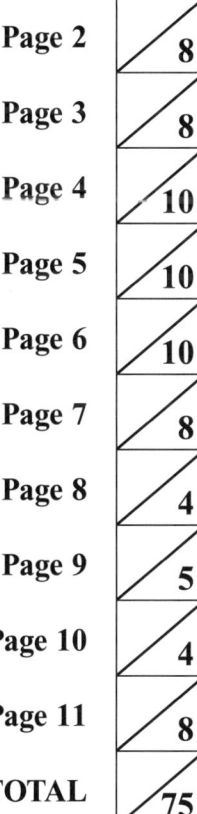

Page 2	8
Page 3	8
Page 4	10
Page 5	10
Page 6	10
Page 7	8
Page 8	4
Page 9	5
Page 10	4
Page 11	8
TOTAL	75

Web: - www.learningtogether.co.uk

Online 11+ platform: - www.onlineelevenplusexams.co.uk

Test Two Page 13

©www.learningtogether.co.uk. For single personal use only.
Copying in any format whatsoever is strictly illegal and will be pursued in courts of law.

LEARNING TOGETHER

CEM NON-VERBAL REASONING
PRACTICE TEST 3

ADVICE AND INSTRUCTIONS ON COMPLETING THIS TEST

(THIS PRACTICE TEST MUST BE COMPLETED IN THE STANDARD FORMAT WAY)

1. There are 75 questions in this test.

2. Start at question 1 and work your way to question 75.

3. If you are unable to complete a question leave it and go to the next one.

4. Do not think about the question you have just left as this wastes time.

5. If you change an answer make sure the change is clear.

6. If there is time left, review your answers and go back and answer any questions that you missed.

7. You may do any rough work on the test paper or on another piece of paper.

8. This test provides practice in the various question types that your child may meet and therefore no time limit has been set.

9. This test reflects the type of non-verbal reasoning questions set by CEM but we cannot guarantee that the 11+ exam your child takes will have the same layout or content as this practice test.

10. An adult may be able to explain any questions you do not understand.

Published by Learning Together 11+ Publishers Ltd, 18 Shandon Park, Belfast, BT5 6NW. Phone/fax 028 90402086
e-mail: online@learningtogether.co.uk. Website:- www.learningtogether.co.uk Online Platform:- www.onlineelevenplusexams.co.uk
All rights reserved. No part of this publication, in whole or in part, may be reproduced, stored in a retrieval system or transmitted, in any form, or by any means, electronic, mechanical, photycoping, recording or otherwise, without the prior written consent of the copyright owner.
Whilst the content of this test is believed to be true and accurate at the time of going to press, neither the authors nor publishers can accept any legal responsibility or liability for any errors or omissions that may have been made.
THE COPYRIGHT OF THIS TEST WILL BE FORCEFULLY DEFENDED IN COURT.

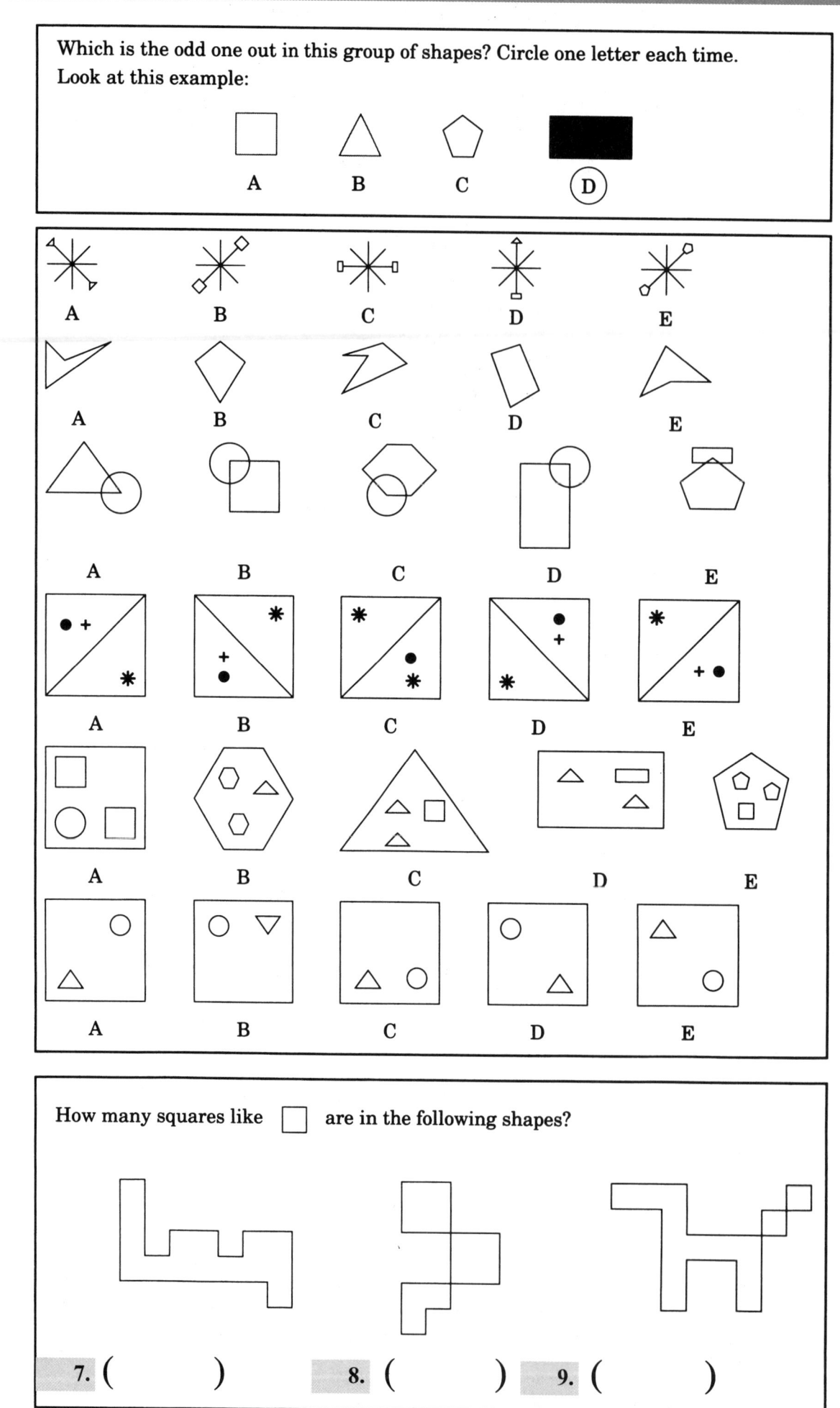

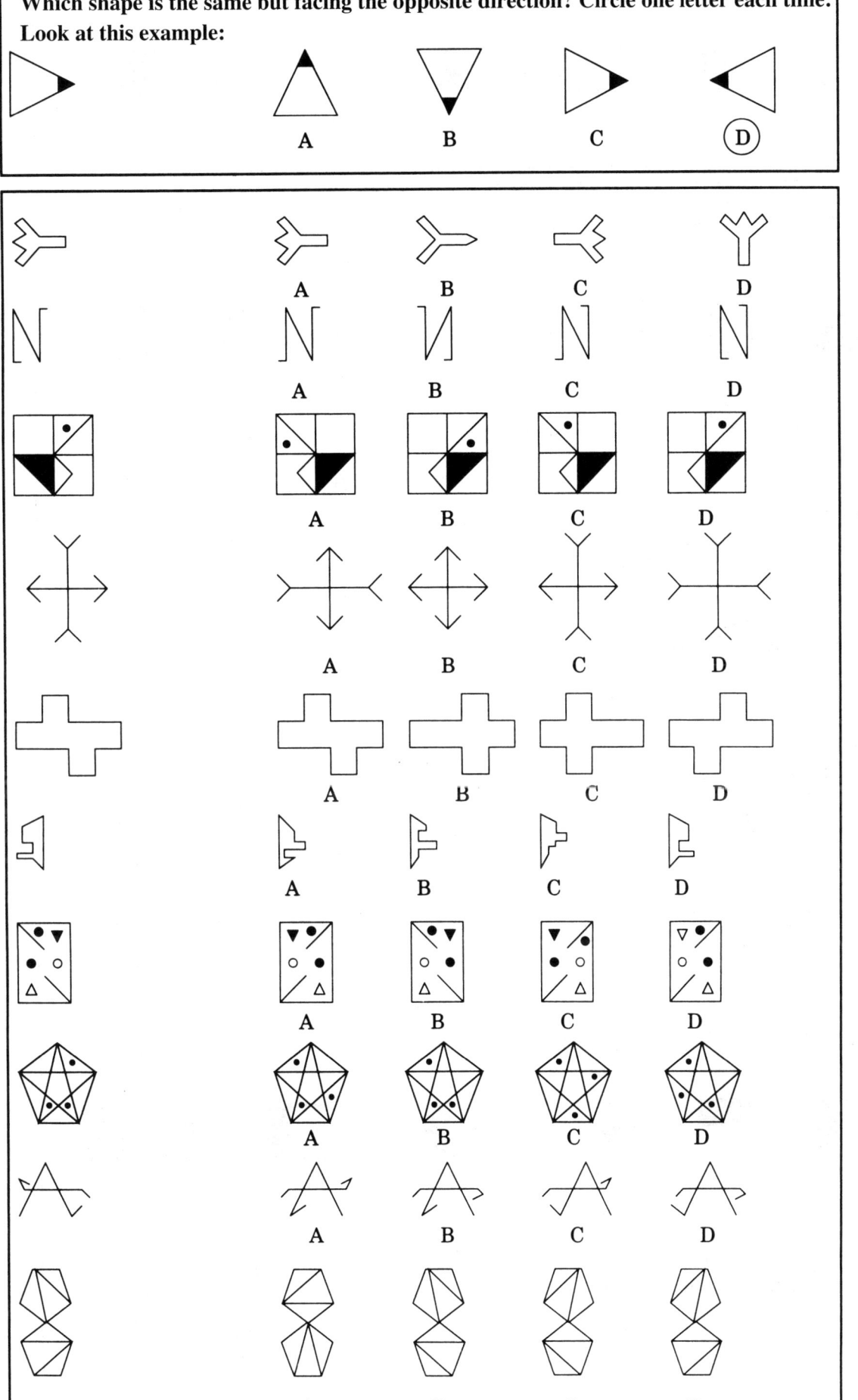

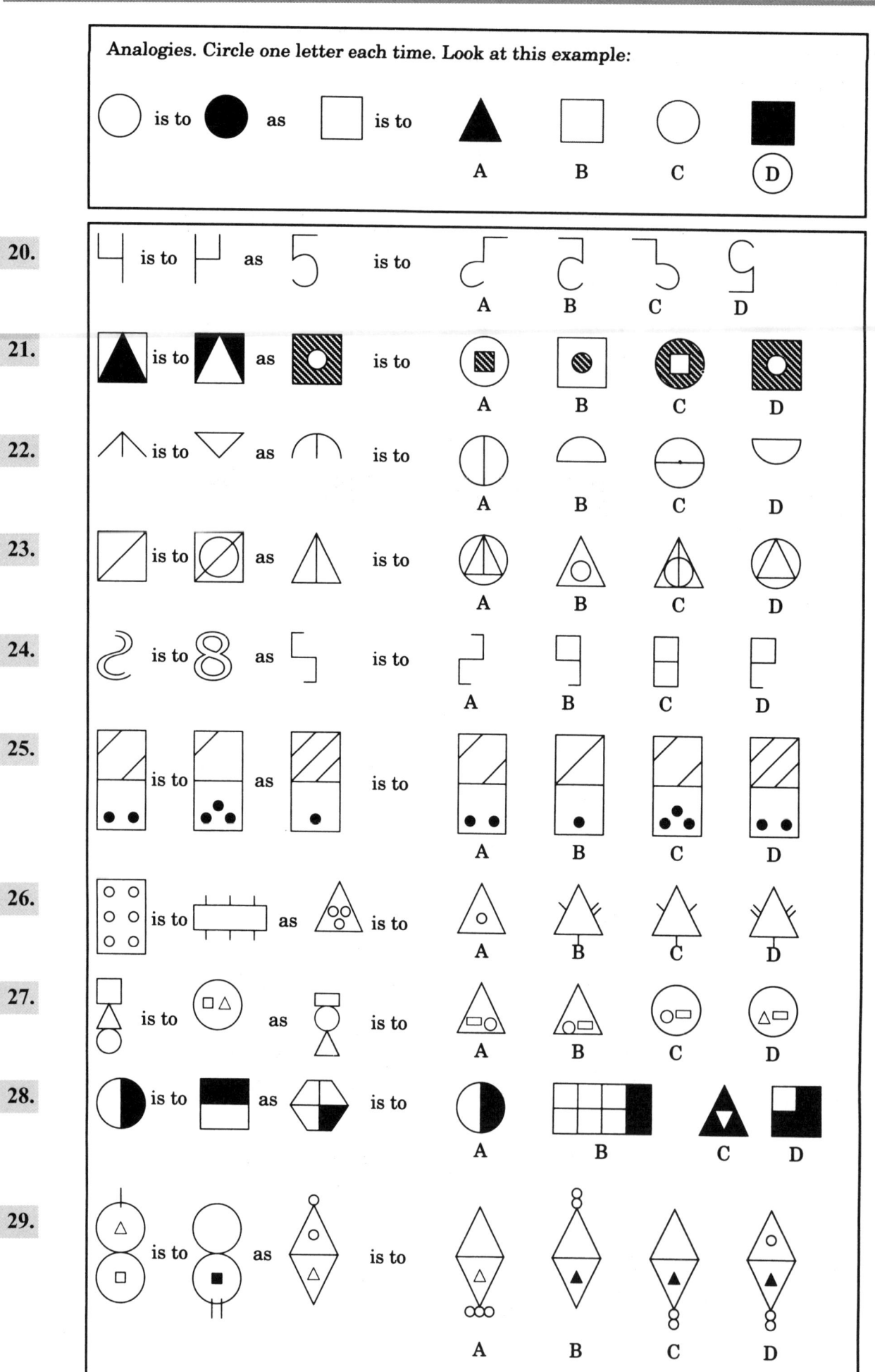

Which two are exactly the same? Circle two letters each time.

30. A B C D E

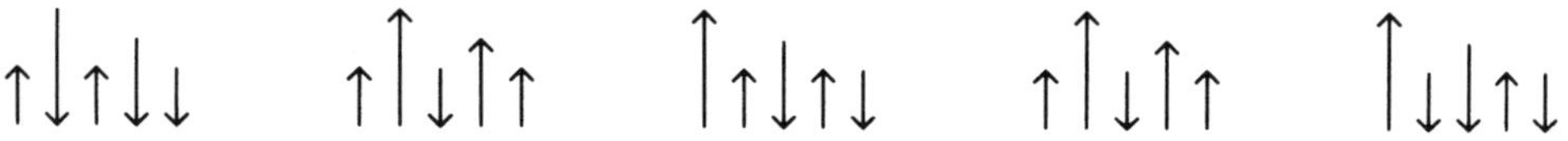

31. A B C D E

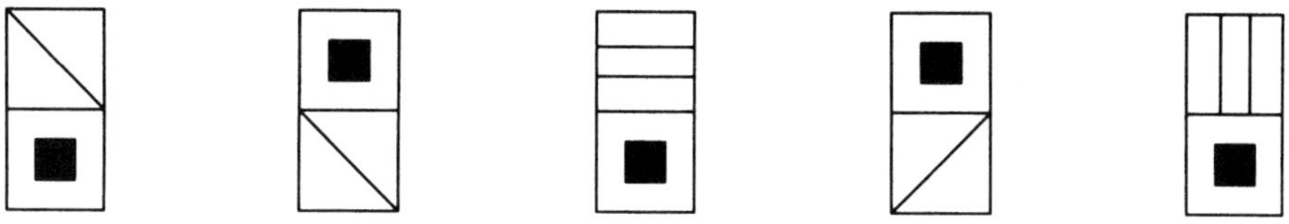

32. A B C D E

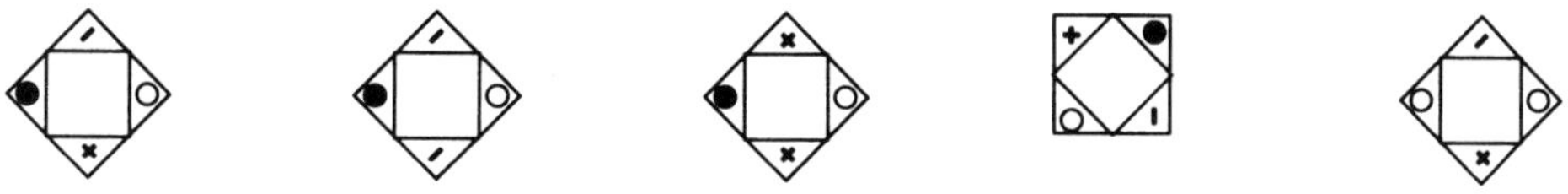

33. A B C D E

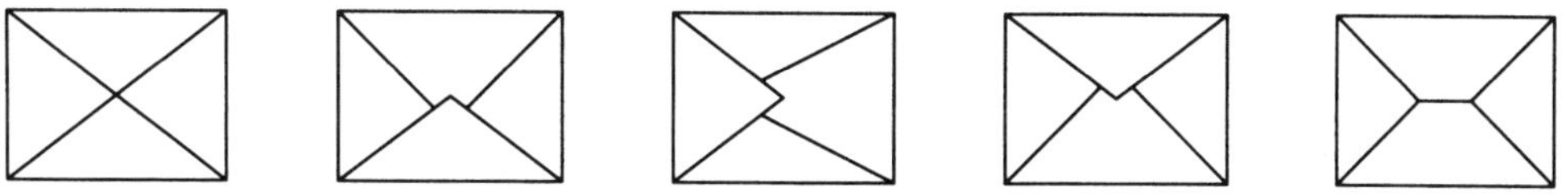

34. A B C D E

35. A B C D E

36. A B C D E

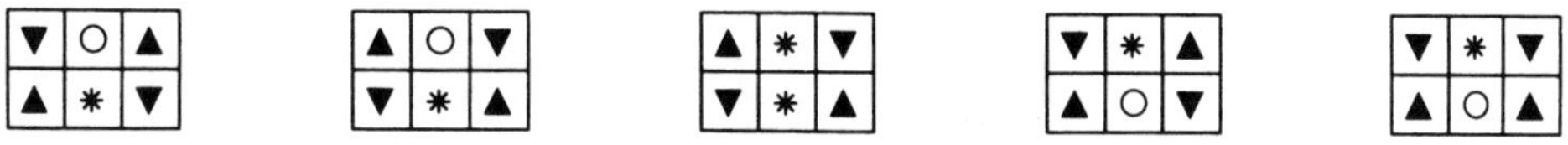

37. A B C D E

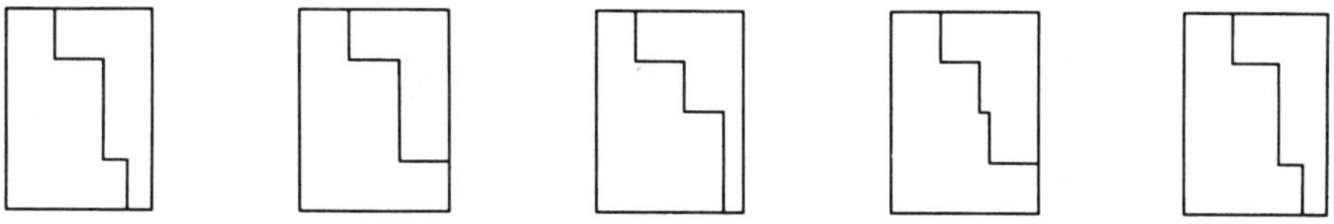

38. A B C D E

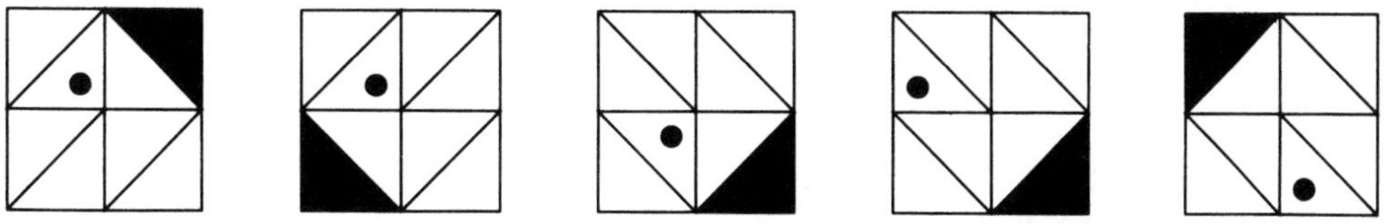

Which larger shape is the small shape hidden in? Circle one letter each time.
Look at this example:

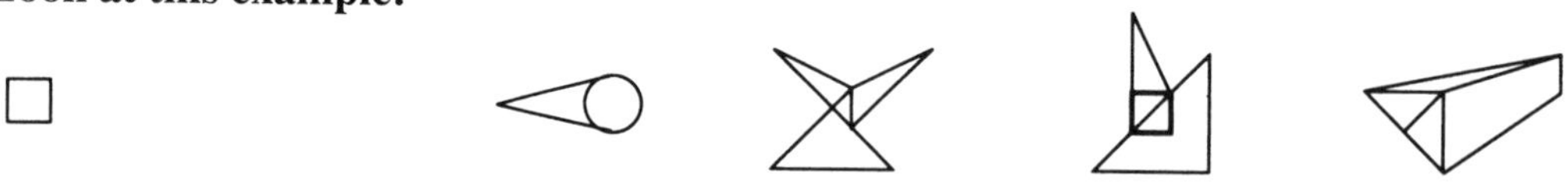

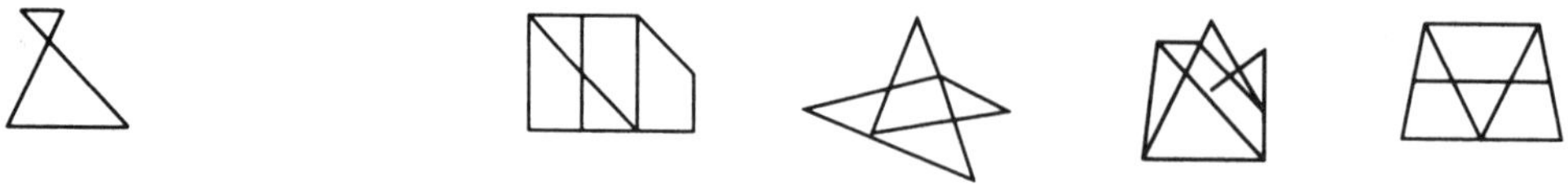

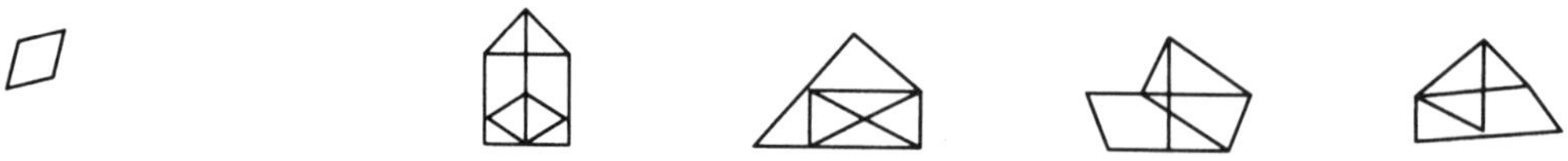

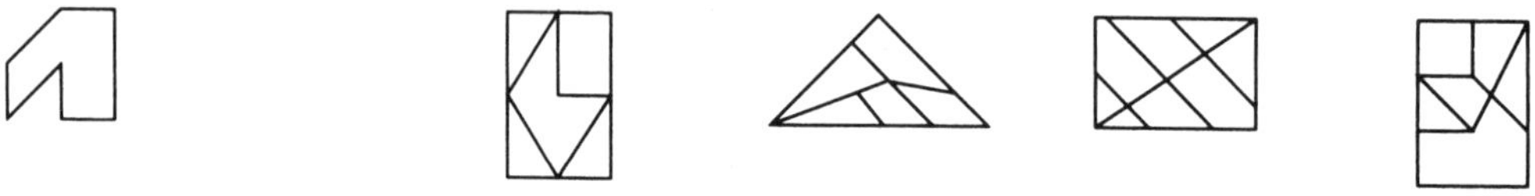

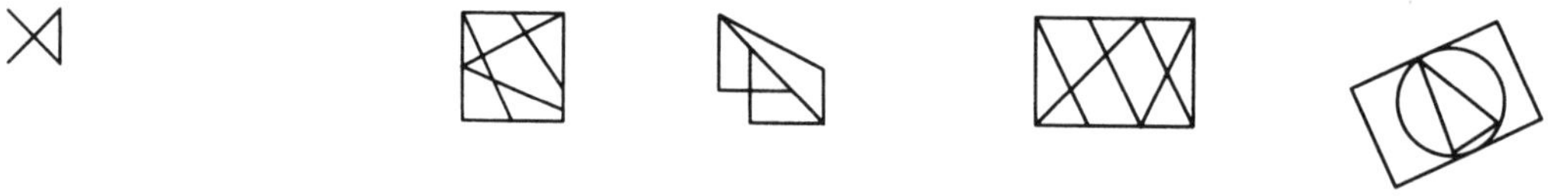

39.
40.
41.
42.
43.

One of the **smaller shapes** will complete the **grid**.
Decide which is the **correct small shape.** Circle the correct letter.

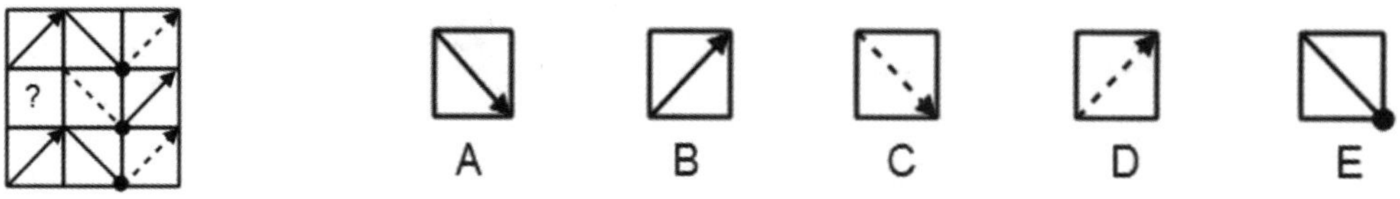

44.
45.
46.
47.

Test Three Page 6

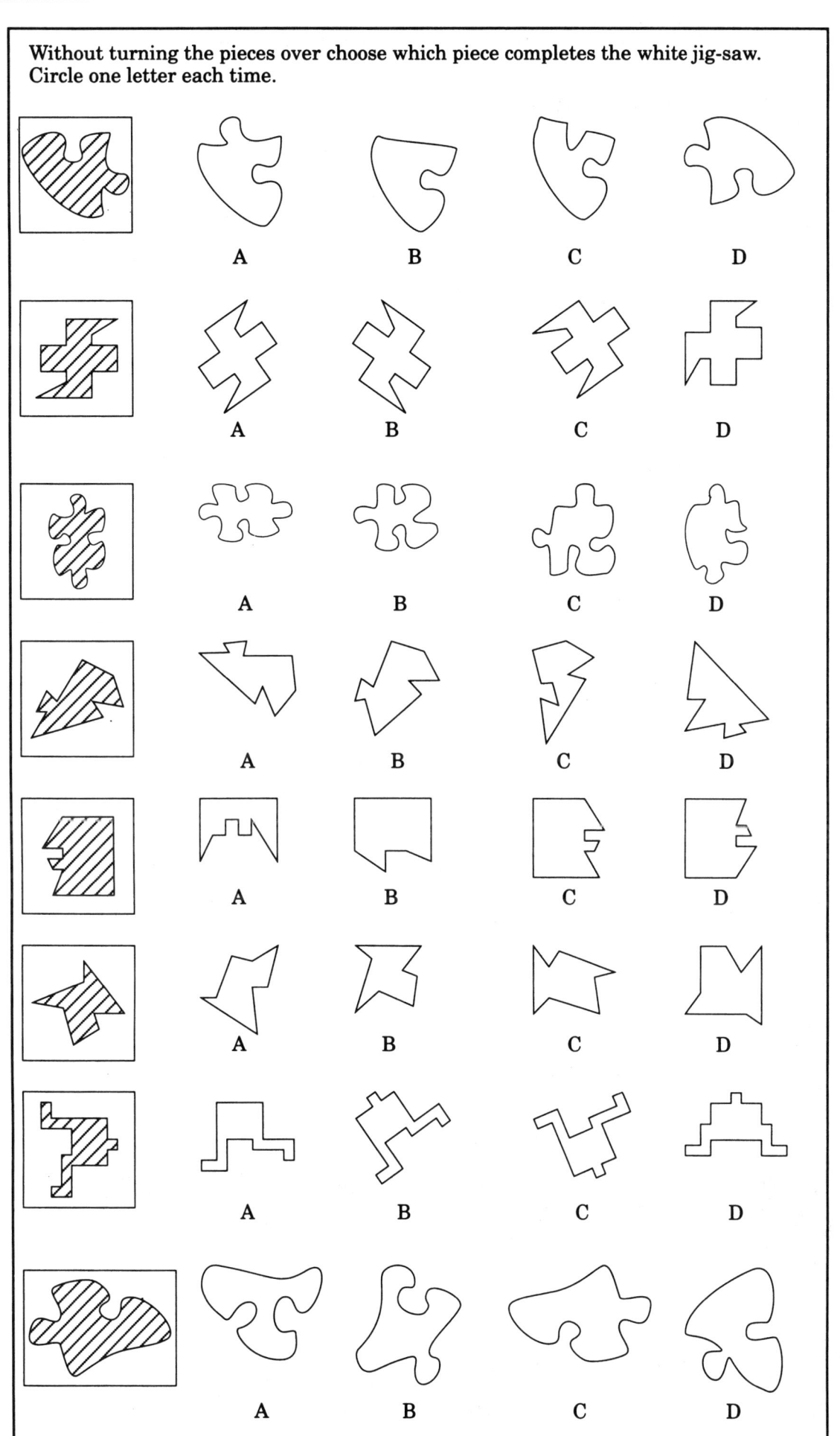

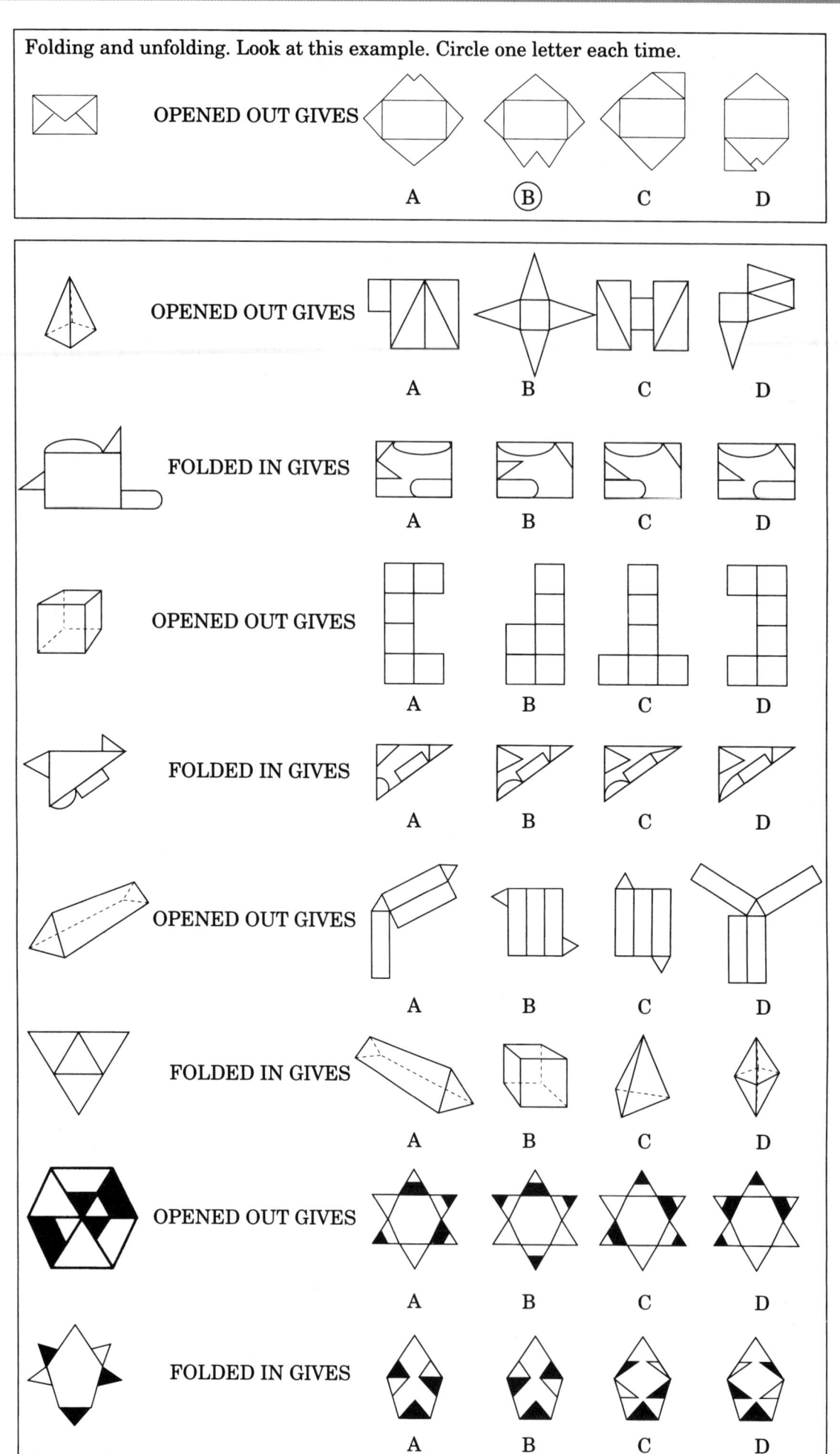

Which shape is different from the other four? Circle one letter each time.

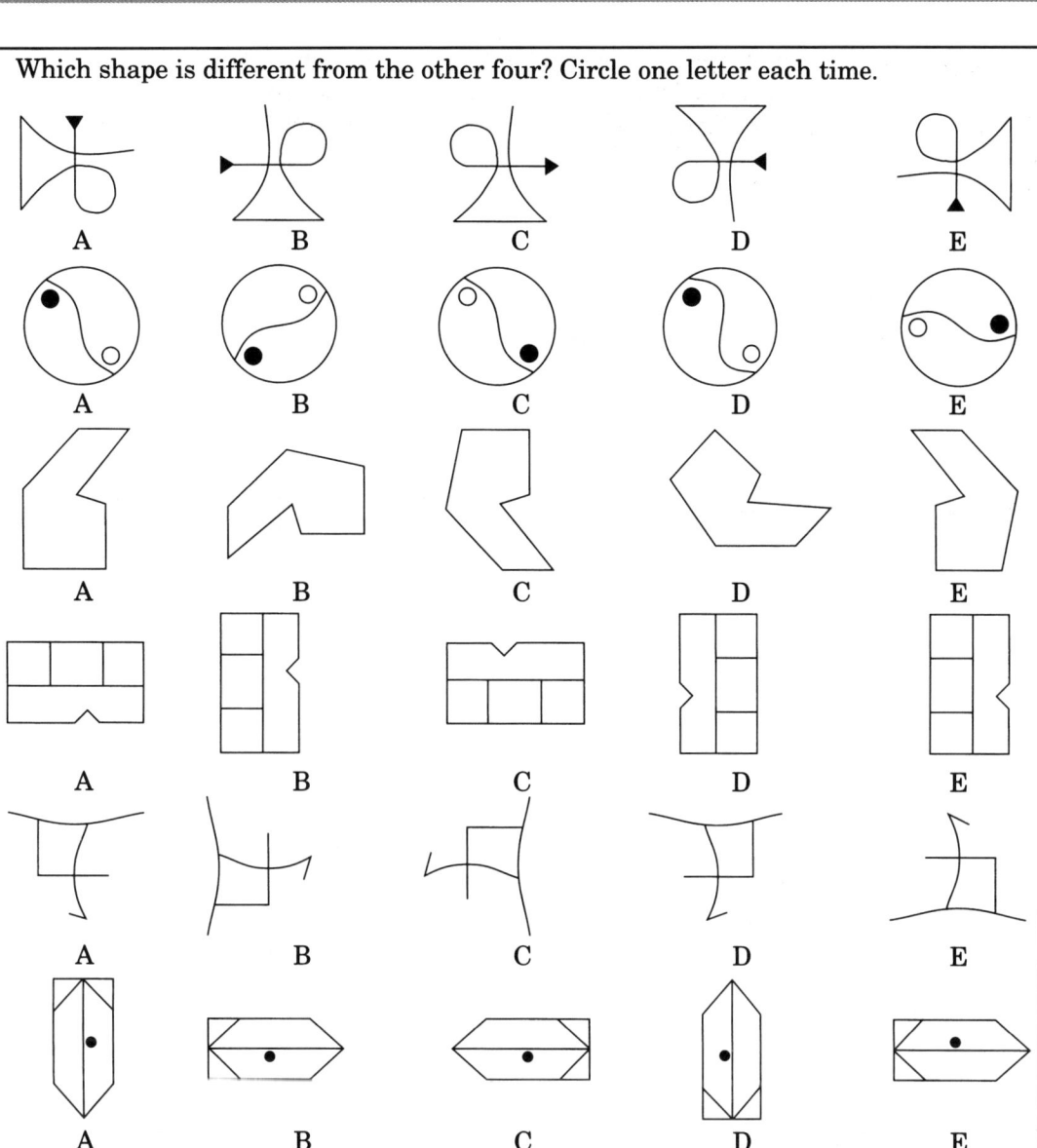

In these questions the two shapes are either added together or subtracted from each other. The shapes do not turn. Circle one answer. Look at this example:

Test Three Page 10

Answers to CEM Non-Verbal Reasoning Practice Test 3.

Question type						
Odd One Out	1	D	Small Shape Hidden	39	C	
	2	C		40	A	
	3	E		41	B	
	4	C		42	D	
	5	D		43	B	
	6	B	Complete 9 Square Grid	44	B	
Count Squares	7	15		45	A	
	8	11		46	E	
	9	14		47	D	
Reflection	10	C	Jigsaws Pieces	48	D	
	11	B		49	A	
	12	C		50	A	
	13	C		51	A	
	14	D		52	D	
	15	D		53	B	
	16	A		54	B	
	17	B		55	C	
	18	C	Folding Shapes	56	B	
	19	C		57	D	
Analogies	20	B		58	C	
	21	B		59	B	
	22	D		60	C	
	23	C		61	C	
	24	C		62	C	
	25	A		63	A	
	26	C	Diferent From Other 4	64	C	
	27	A		65	D	
	28	B		66	A	
	29	C		67	E	
2 Shapes the Same	30	B and D		68	D	
	31	A and B		69	B	
	32	A and D	Adding and Substracting Shapes	70	C	
	33	B and D		71	D	
	34	A and C		72	A	
	35	A and D		73	D	
	36	B and D		74	D	
	37	A and E		75	B	
	38	B and C				

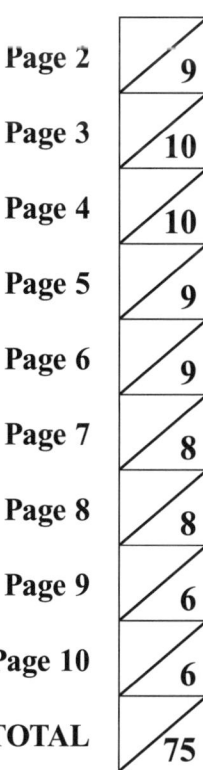

Page 2	9
Page 3	10
Page 4	10
Page 5	9
Page 6	9
Page 7	8
Page 8	8
Page 9	6
Page 10	6
TOTAL	75

Web: - www.learningtogether.co.uk

Online 11+ platform: - www.onlineelevenplusexams.co.uk

Test Three Page 11

©www.learningtogether.co.uk. For single personal use only.
Copying in any format whatsoever is strictly illegal and will be pursued in courts of law.

LEARNING TOGETHER

CEM NON-VERBAL REASONING
PRACTICE TEST 4

ADVICE AND INSTRUCTIONS ON COMPLETING THIS TEST

(THIS PRACTICE TEST MUST BE COMPLETED IN THE STANDARD FORMAT WAY)

1. There are 75 questions in this test.

2. Start at question 1 and work your way to question 75.

3. If you are unable to complete a question leave it and go to the next one.

4. Do not think about the question you have just left as this wastes time.

5. If you change an answer make sure the change is clear.

6. If there is time left, review your answers and go back and answer any questions that you missed.

7. You may do any rough work on the test paper or on another piece of paper.

8. This test provides practice in the various question types that your child may meet and therefore no time limit has been set.

9. This test reflects the type of non-verbal reasoning questions set by CEM but we cannot guarantee that the 11+ exam your child takes will have the same layout or content as this practice test.

10. An adult may be able to explain any questions you do not understand.

Published by Learning Together 11+ Publishers Ltd, 18 Shandon Park, Belfast, BT5 6NW. Phone/fax 028 90402086
e-mail: online@learningtogether.co.uk Website:- www.learningtogether.co.uk Online Platform:- www.onlineelevenplusexams.co.uk

All rights reserved. No part of this publication, in whole or in part, may be reproduced, stored in a retrieval system or transmitted, in any form, or by any means, electronic, mechanical, photycoping, recording or otherwise, without the prior written consent of the copyright owner.

Whilst the content of this test is believed to be true and accurate at the time of going to press, neither the authors nor publishers can accept any legal responsibility or liability for any errors or omissions that may have been made.
THE COPYRIGHT OF THIS TEST WILL BE FORCEFULLY DEFENDED IN COURT.

There are two **similar shapes** on the **left**.
Which **shape** on the **right** is **similar** to the **two shapes on the left**?
Circle the correct letter.

1.   A   B   C   D   E

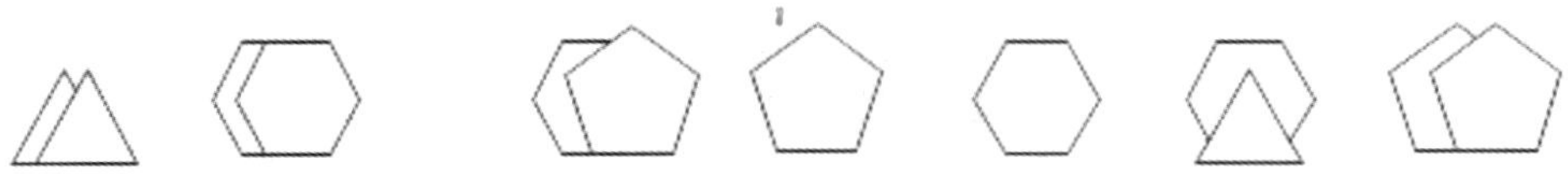

2.   A   B   C   D   E

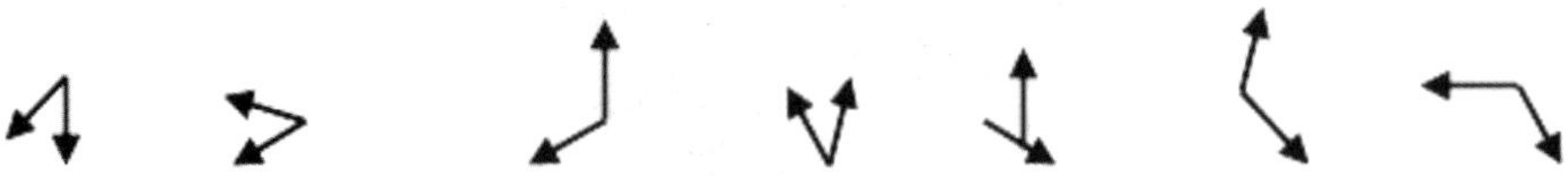

3.   A   B   C   D   E

4.   A   B   C   D   E

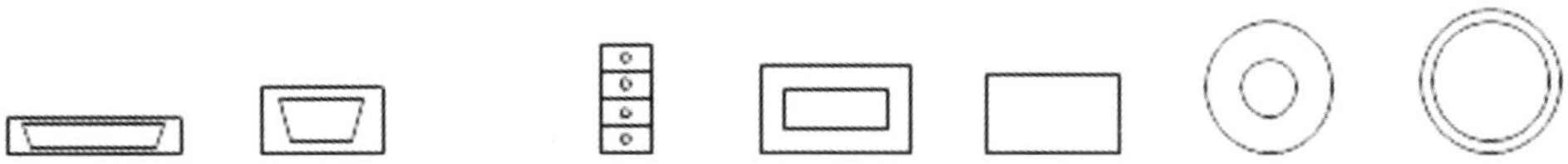

5.   A   B   C   D   E

6.   A   B   C   D   E

7.   A   B   C   D   E

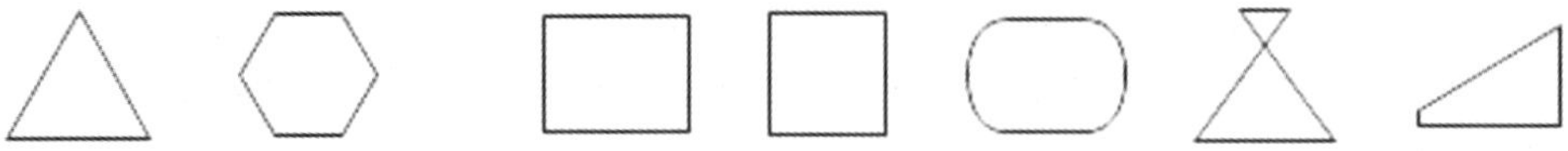

8.   A   B   C   D   E

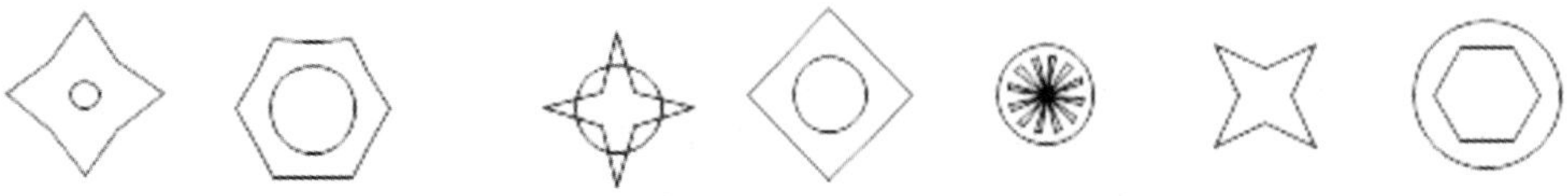

Test Four Page 2

Which larger shape is the small shape hidden in? Circle one letter each time.
Look at this example.

9. is hidden in   A   B   C   D

10. is hidden in   A   B   C   D

11. is hidden in   A   B   C   D

12. is hidden in   A   B   C   D

Test Four Page 3

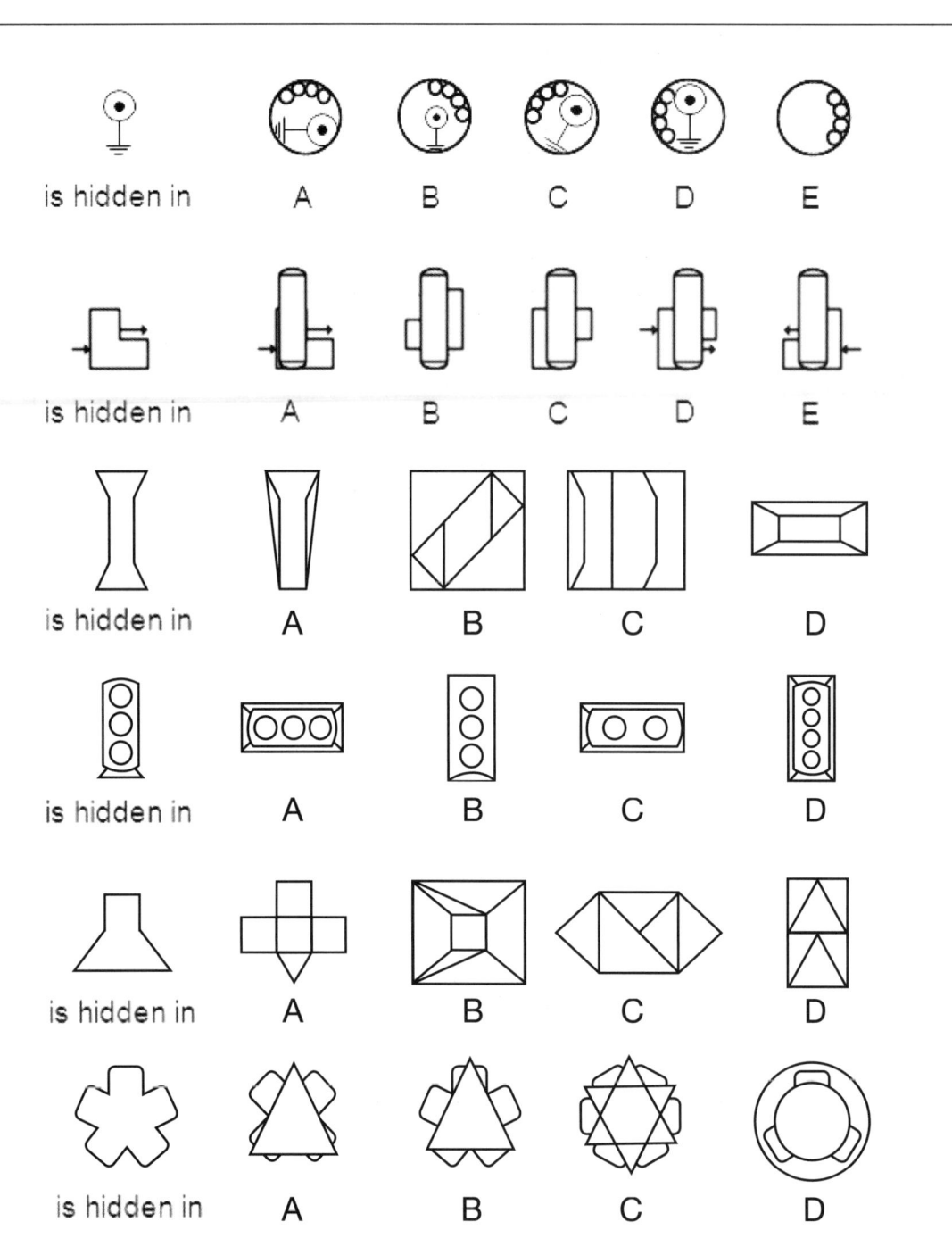

In these questions the two shapes are either added together or subtracted from each other. The shapes do not turn. Circle one answer. Look at this example:

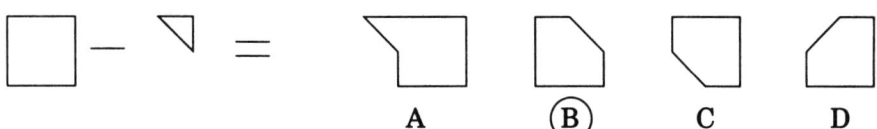

19.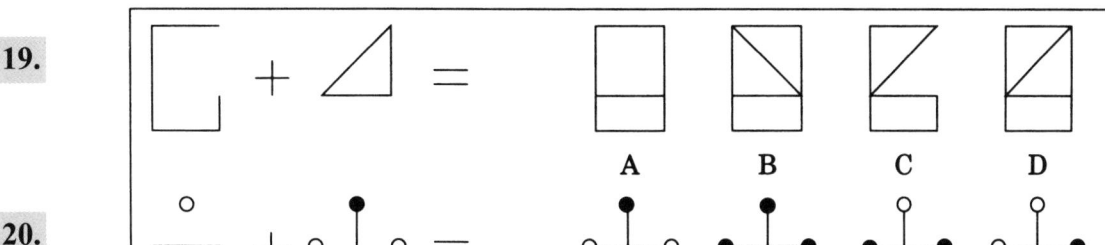

20.

21.

22.

23.

24.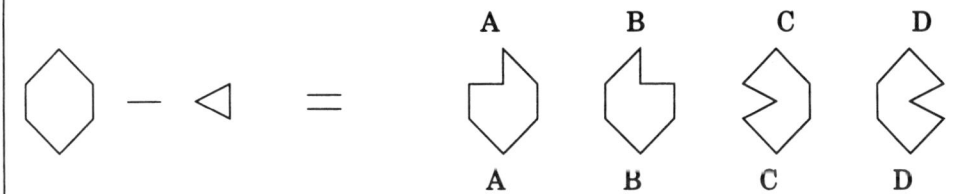

25.

26.

27.

28.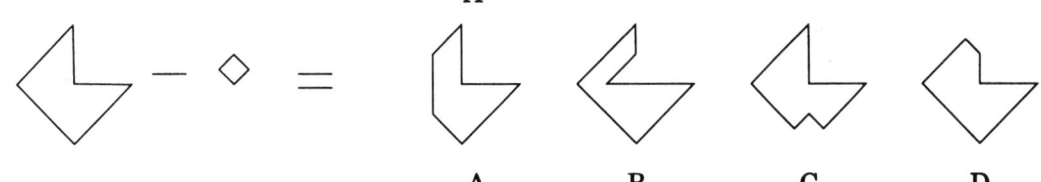

Test Four Page 5

Which is the odd one out in this group of shapes? Circle one letter each time
Look at this example

A   B   C   D

29. A   B   C   D

30. A   B   C   D

31. A   B   C   D   E

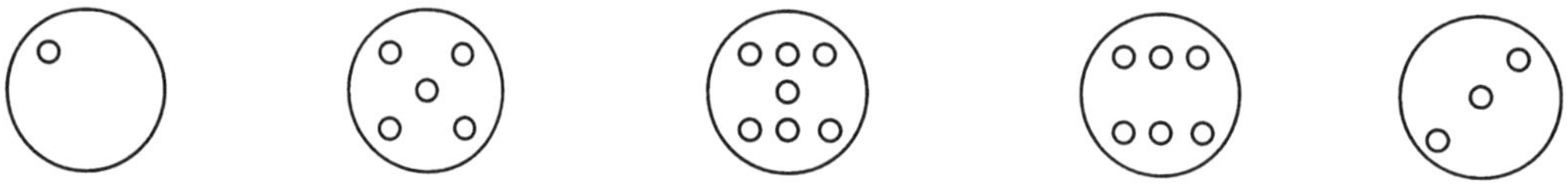

32. A   B   C   D   E

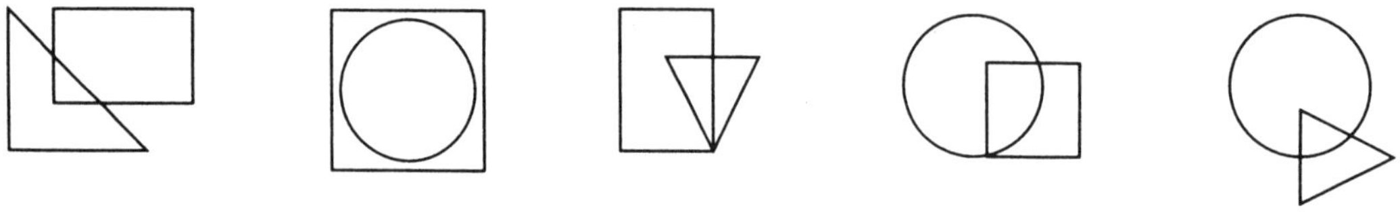

33. A   B   C   D   E

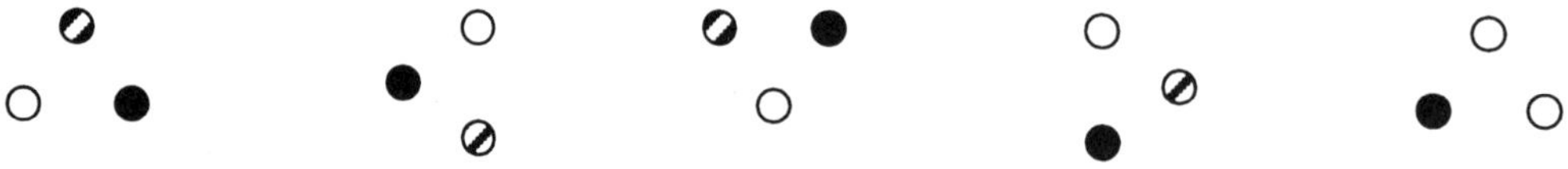

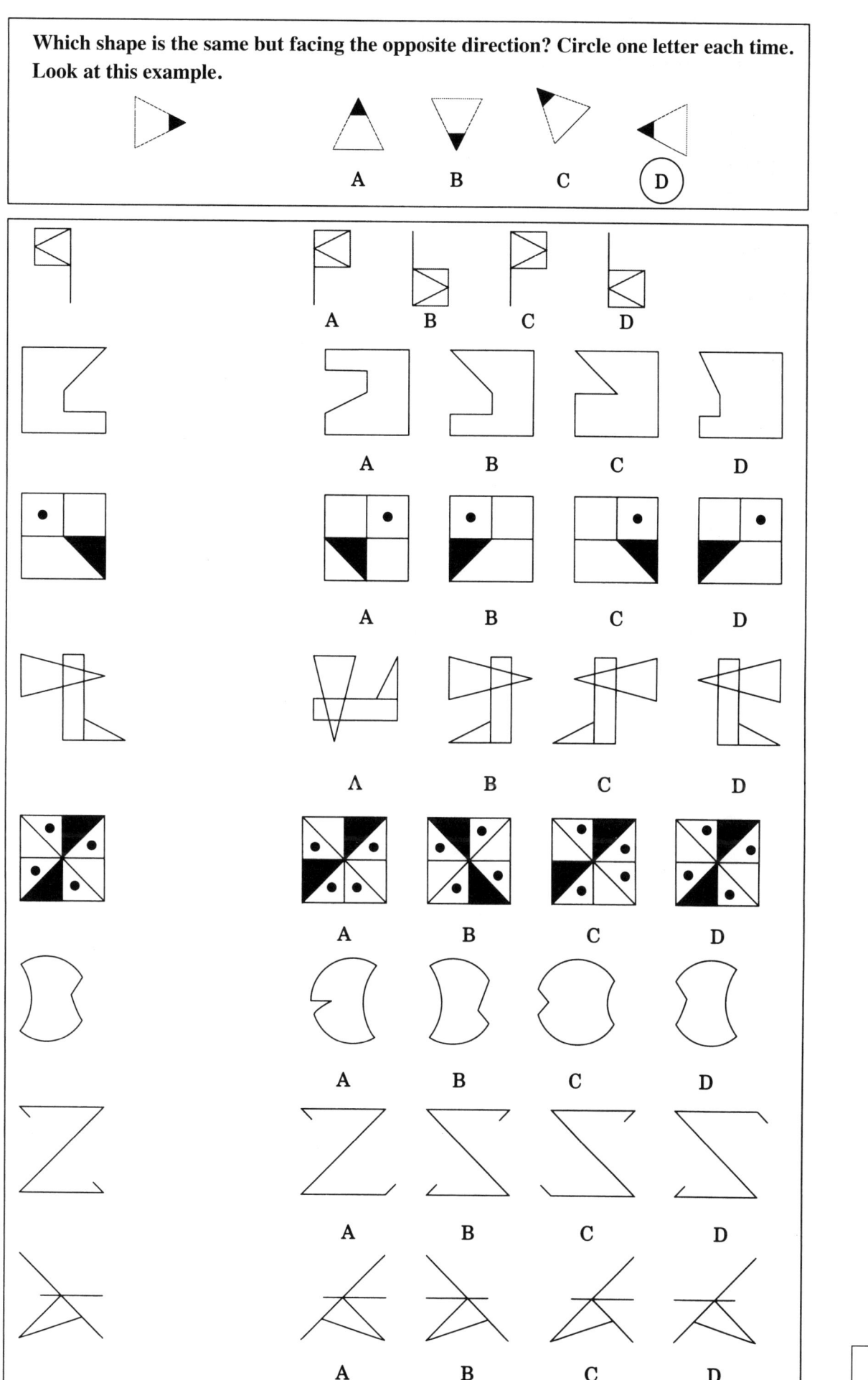

Without turning the pieces over choose which piece completes the white jig-saw. Circle one letter each time.

42. A   B   C   D

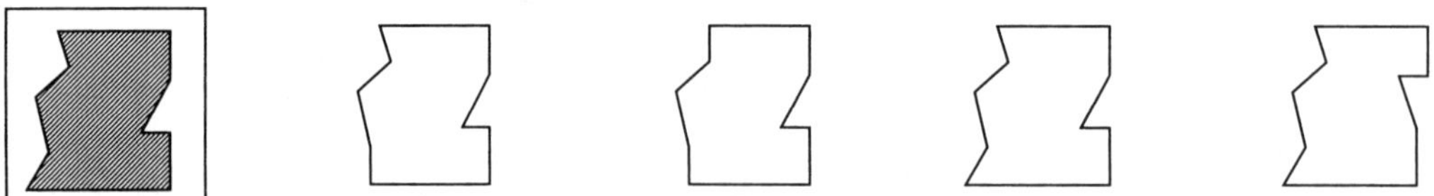

43. A   B   C   D

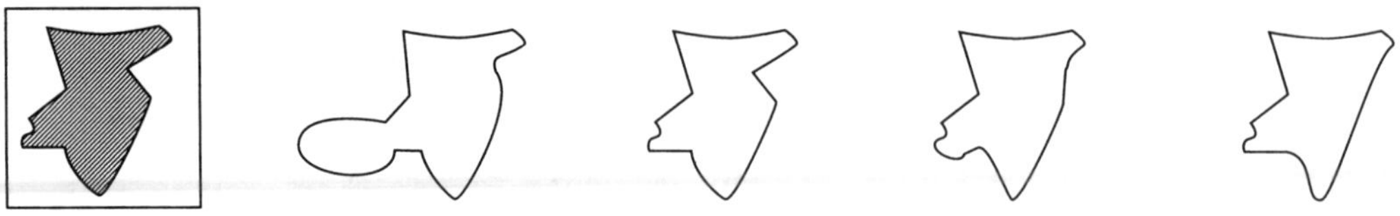

44. A   B   C   D

45. A   B   C   D

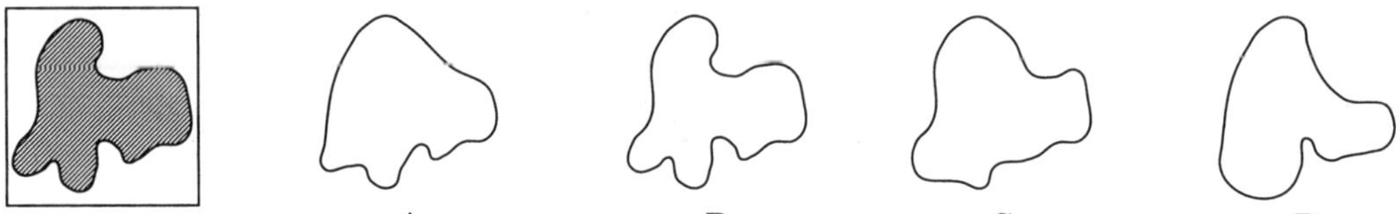

Test Four Page 8

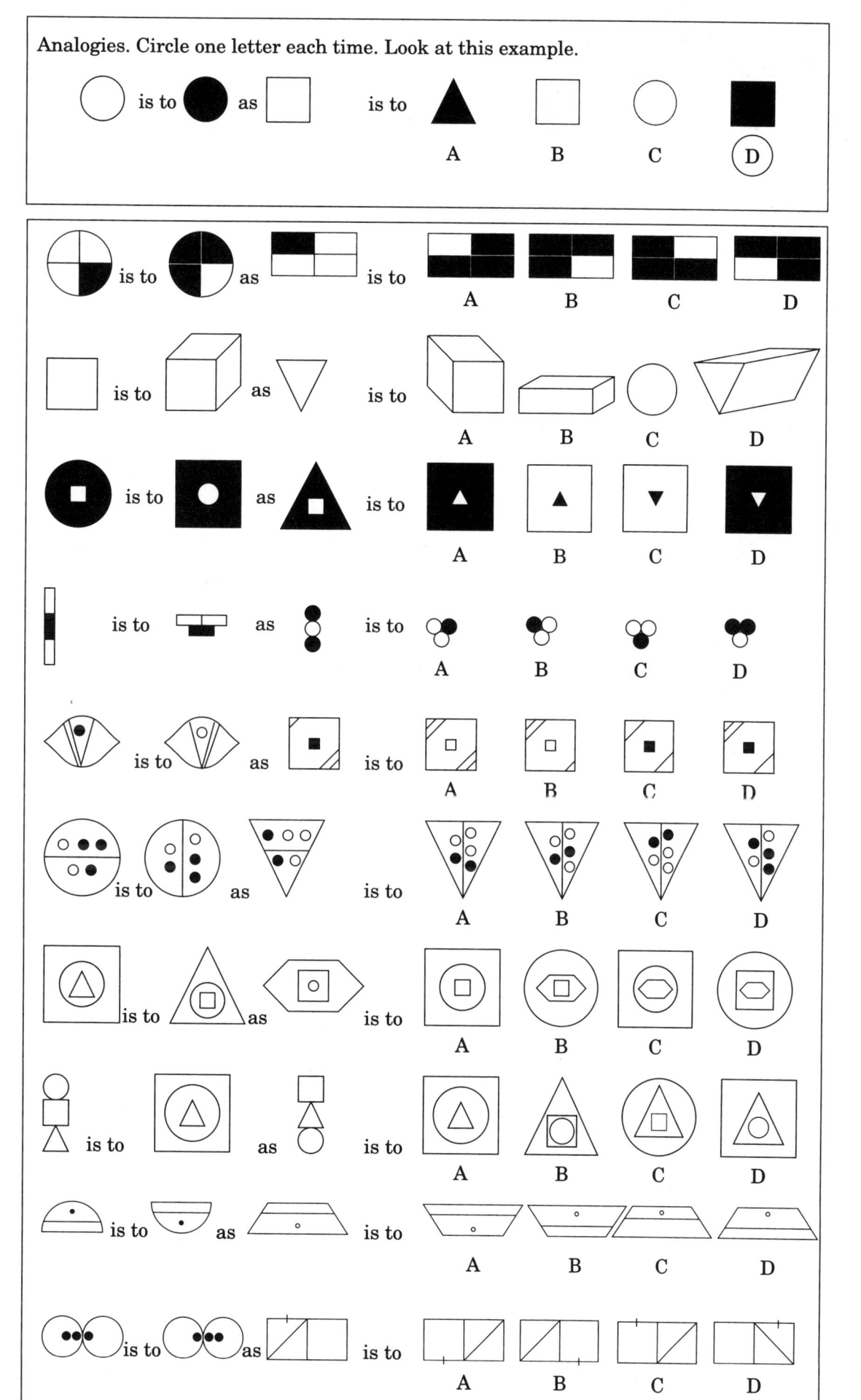

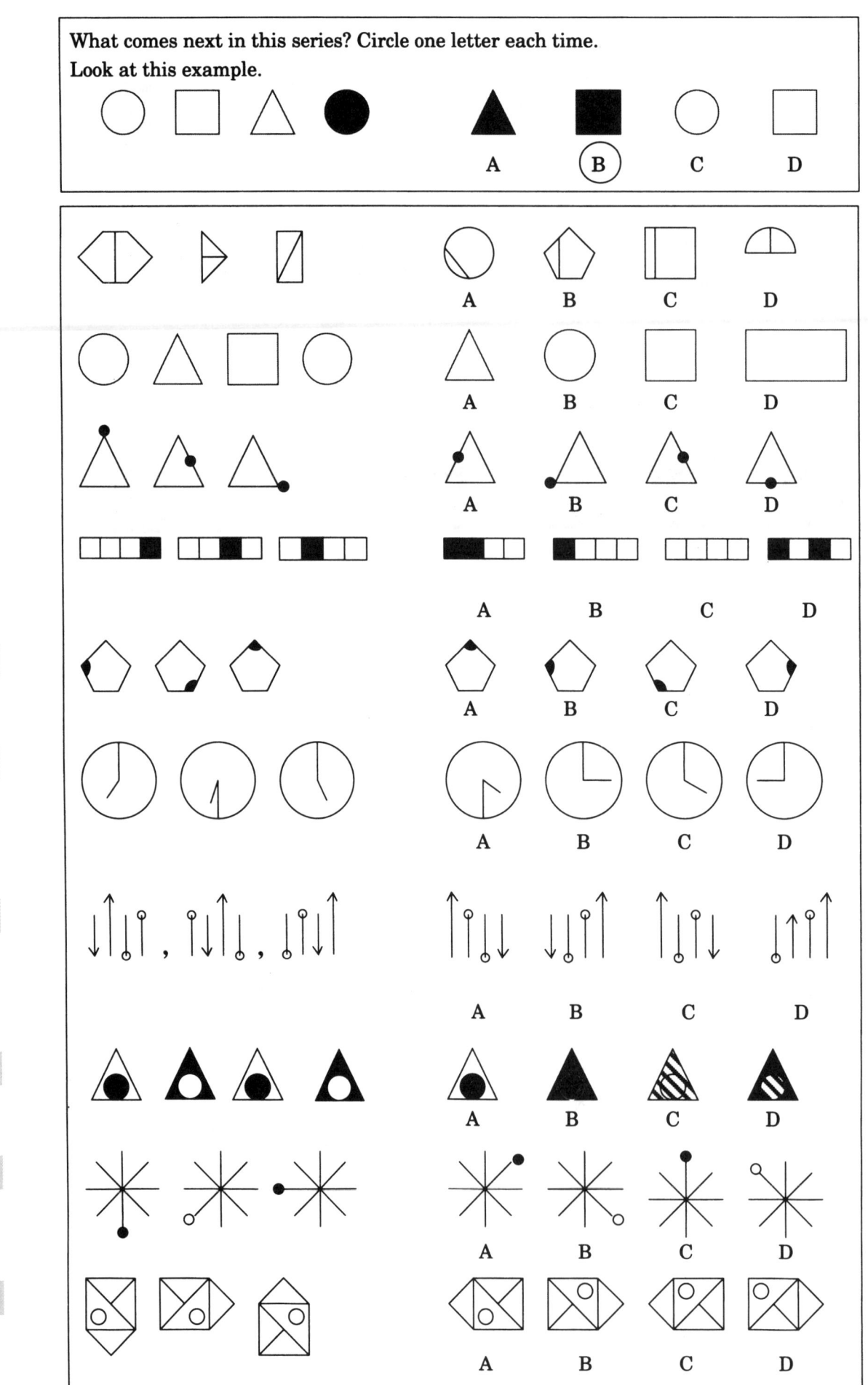

Which two are exactly the same. Circle two letters each time.

66. A B C D E F

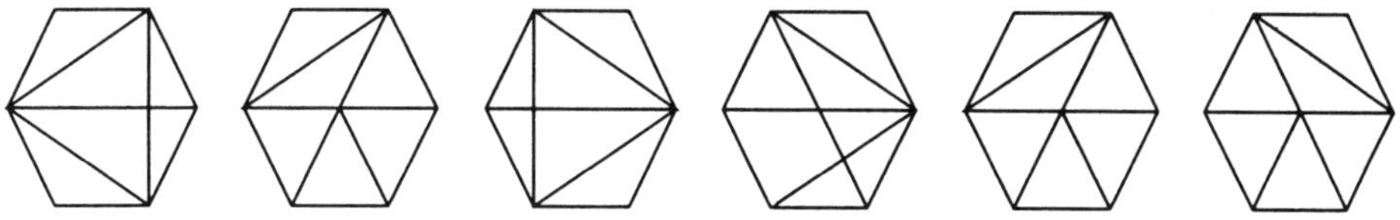

67. A B C D E F

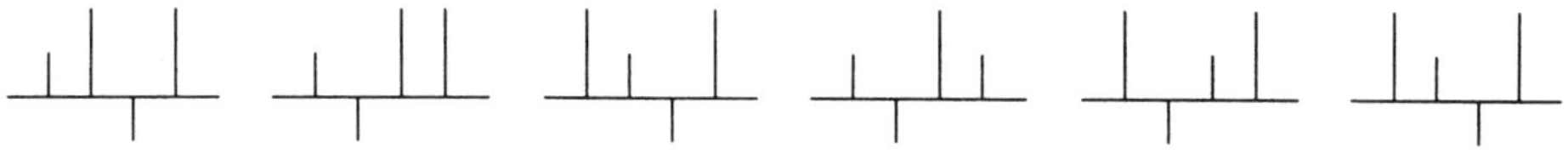

68. A B C D E F

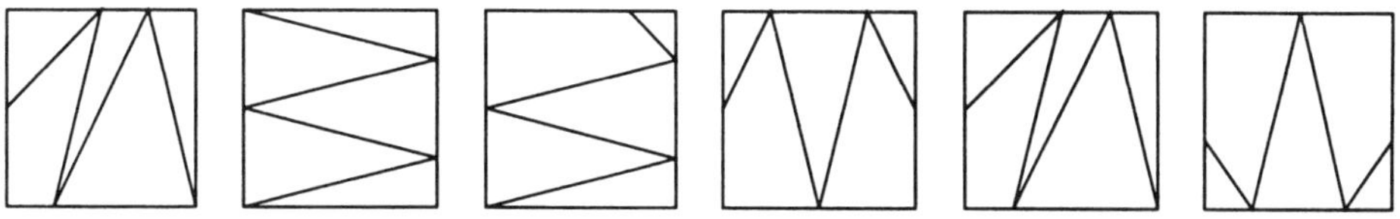

69. A B C D E F

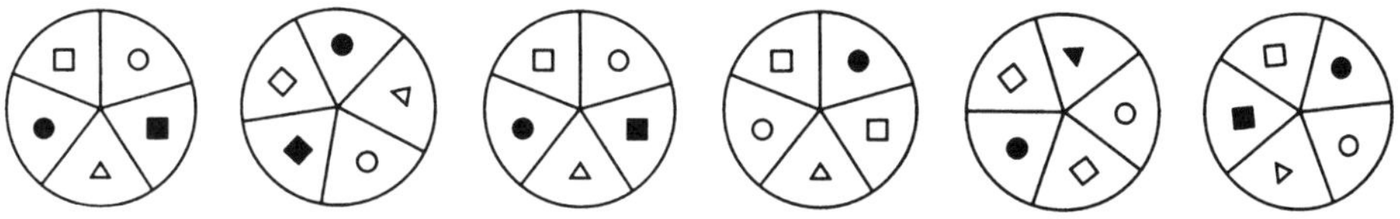

70. A B C D E F

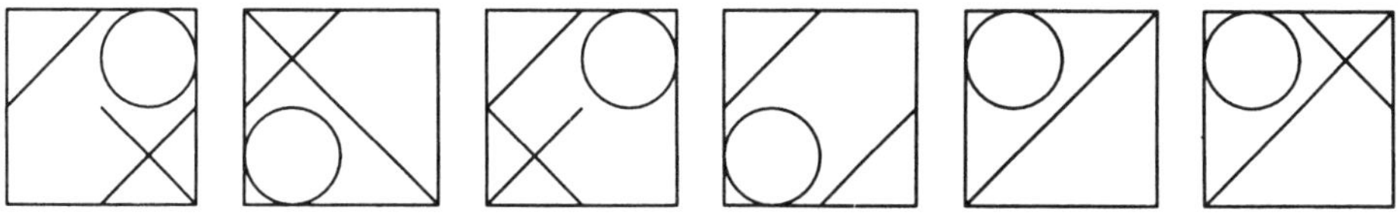

71. A B C D E F

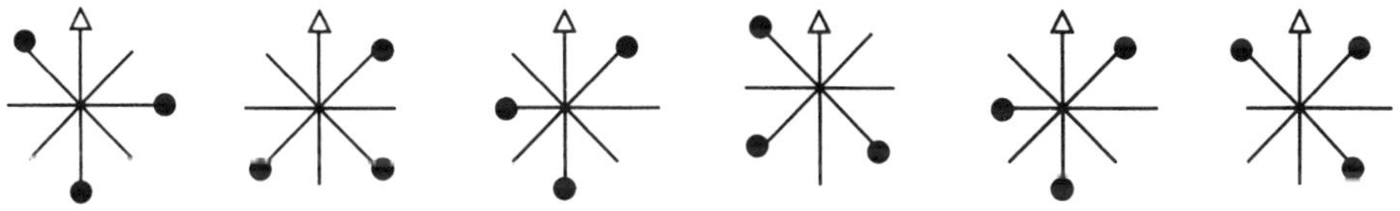

One of the smaller shapes will complete the grid.
Decide which is the correct small shape. Circle the correct letter.

72. A B C D E

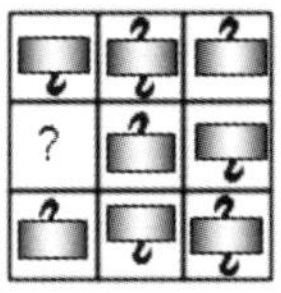

73. A B C D E

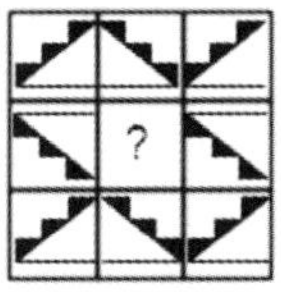

74. A B C D E

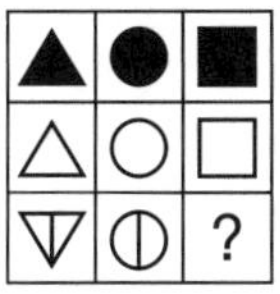

75. A B C D E

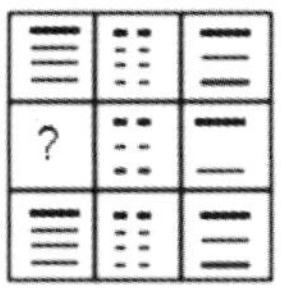

Test Four Page 11

Answers to CEM Non-Verbal Reasoning Practice Test 4.

Question type						
Similar to Two Shapes	1	E	Reflection	39	D	
	2	B		40	B	
	3	C		41	D	
	4	B	Jigsaw	42	C	
	5	A		43	B	
	6	C		44	C	
	7	B		45	B	
Hidden Shape	8	B	Analogies	46	A	
	9	C		47	D	
	10	D		48	A	
	11	A		49	D	
	12	B		50	B	
	13	D		51	C	
	14	A		52	D	
	15	D		53	B	
	16	A		54	B	
	17	B		55	D	
Adding and Substracting Shapes	18	B	Series	56	D	
	19	D		57	A	
	20	A		58	D	
	21	C		59	B	
	22	B		60	C	
	23	D		61	A	
	24	B		62	C	
	25	C		63	A	
	26	C		64	D	
	27	D		65	C	
Odd One Out	28	C	Two the Same	66	B and E	
	29	C		67	C and F	
	30	D		68	A and E	
	31	D		69	A and C	
	32	B		70	B and F	
	33	E		71	C and E	
Reflection	34	C	A Square Grid	72	B	
	35	B		73	D	
	36	D		74	B	
	37	C		75	C	
	38	B				

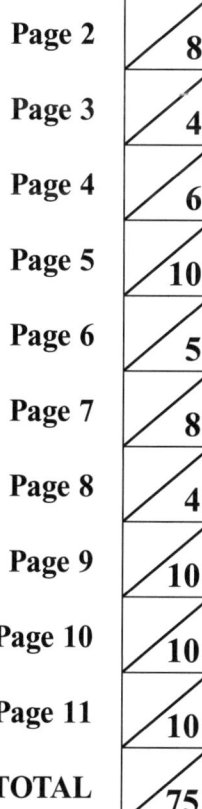

Page 2	8
Page 3	4
Page 4	6
Page 5	10
Page 6	5
Page 7	8
Page 8	4
Page 9	10
Page 10	10
Page 11	10
TOTAL	75

Web: - www.learningtogether.co.uk

Online 11+ platform: - www.onlineelevenplusexams.co.uk

Test Four Page 13

©www.learningtogether.co.uk. For single personal use only.
Copying in any format whatsoever is strictly illegal and will be pursued in courts of law.

LEARNING TOGETHER

CEM NON-VERBAL REASONING
PRACTICE TEST 5

ADVICE AND INSTRUCTIONS ON COMPLETING THIS TEST

(THIS PRACTICE TEST MUST BE COMPLETED IN THE STANDARD FORMAT WAY)

1. There are 75 questions in this test.

2. Start at question 1 and work your way to question 75.

3. If you are unable to complete a question leave it and go to the next one.

4. Do not think about the question you have just left as this wastes time.

5. If you change an answer make sure the change is clear.

6. If there is time left, review your answers and go back and answer any questions that you missed.

7. You may do any rough work on the test paper or on another piece of paper.

8. This test provides practice in the various question types that your child may meet and therefore no time limit has been set.

9. This test reflects the type of non-verbal reasoning questions set by CEM but we cannot guarantee that the 11+ exam your child takes will have the same layout or content as this practice test.

10. An adult may be able to explain any questions you do not understand.

Published by Learning Together 11+ Publishers Ltd, 18 Shandon Park, Belfast, BT5 6NW. Phone/fax 028 90402086
e-mail: online@learningtogether.co.uk. Website:- www.learningtogether.co.uk Online Platform:- www.onlineelevenplusexams.co.uk

All rights reserved. No part of this publication, in whole or in part, may be reproduced, stored in a retrieval system or transmitted, in any form, or by any means, electronic, mechanical, photycoping, recording or otherwise, without the prior written consent of the copyright owner.

Whilst the content of this test is believed to be true and accurate at the time of going to press, neither the authors nor publishers can accept any legal responsibility or liability for any errors or omissions that may have been made.
THE COPYRIGHT OF THIS TEST WILL BE FORCEFULLY DEFENDED IN COURT.

Which two are exactly the same? Circle two letters each time.

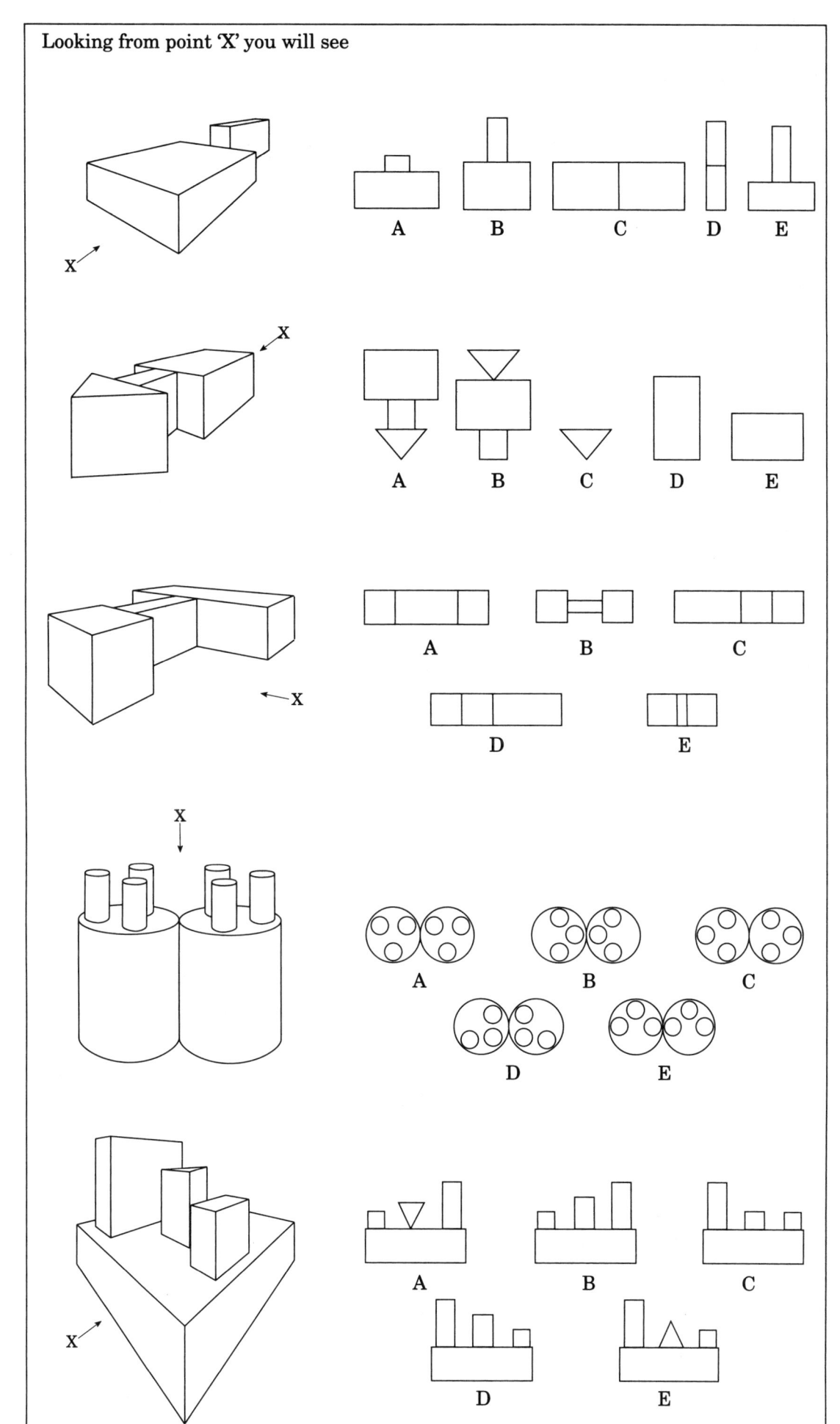

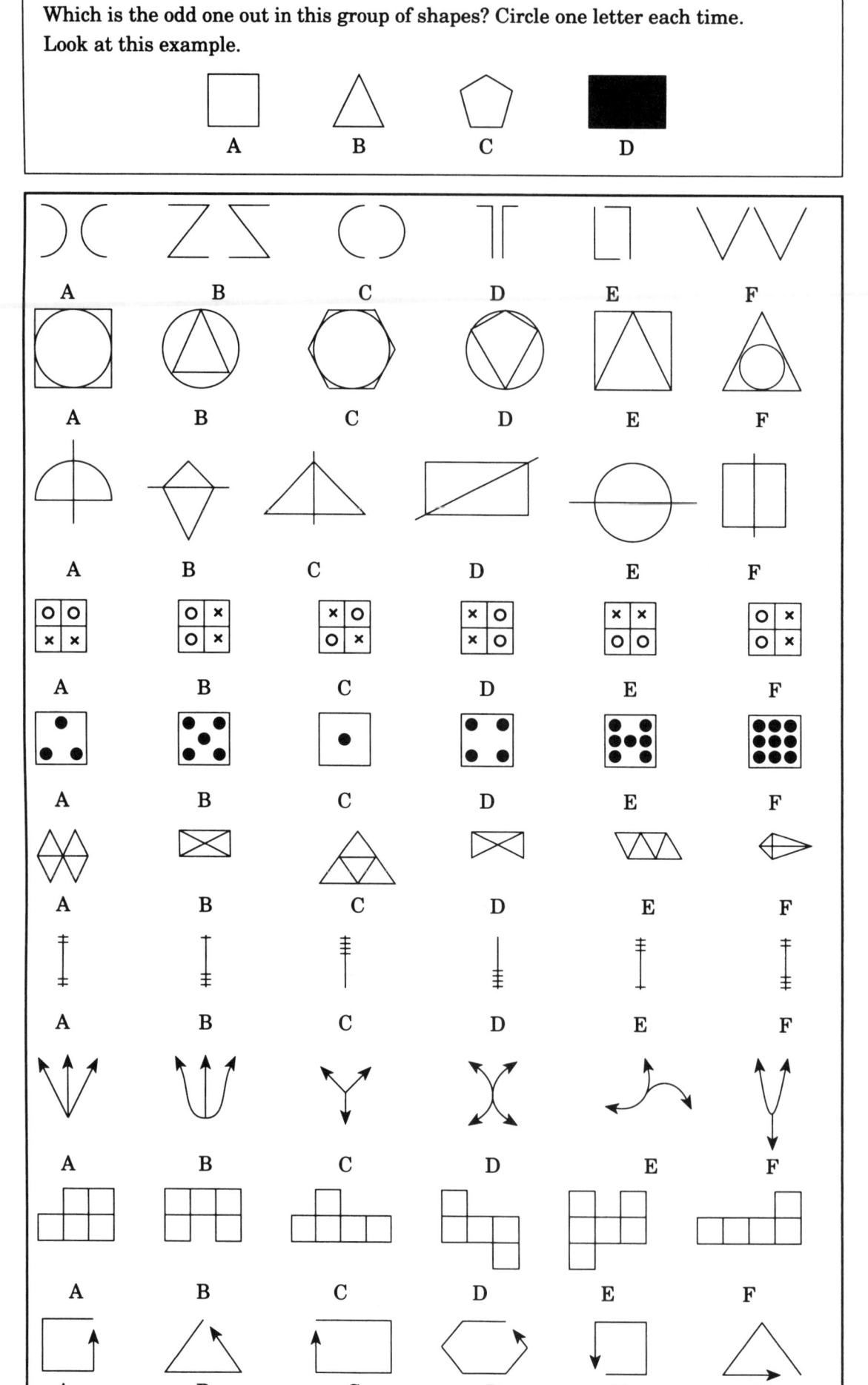

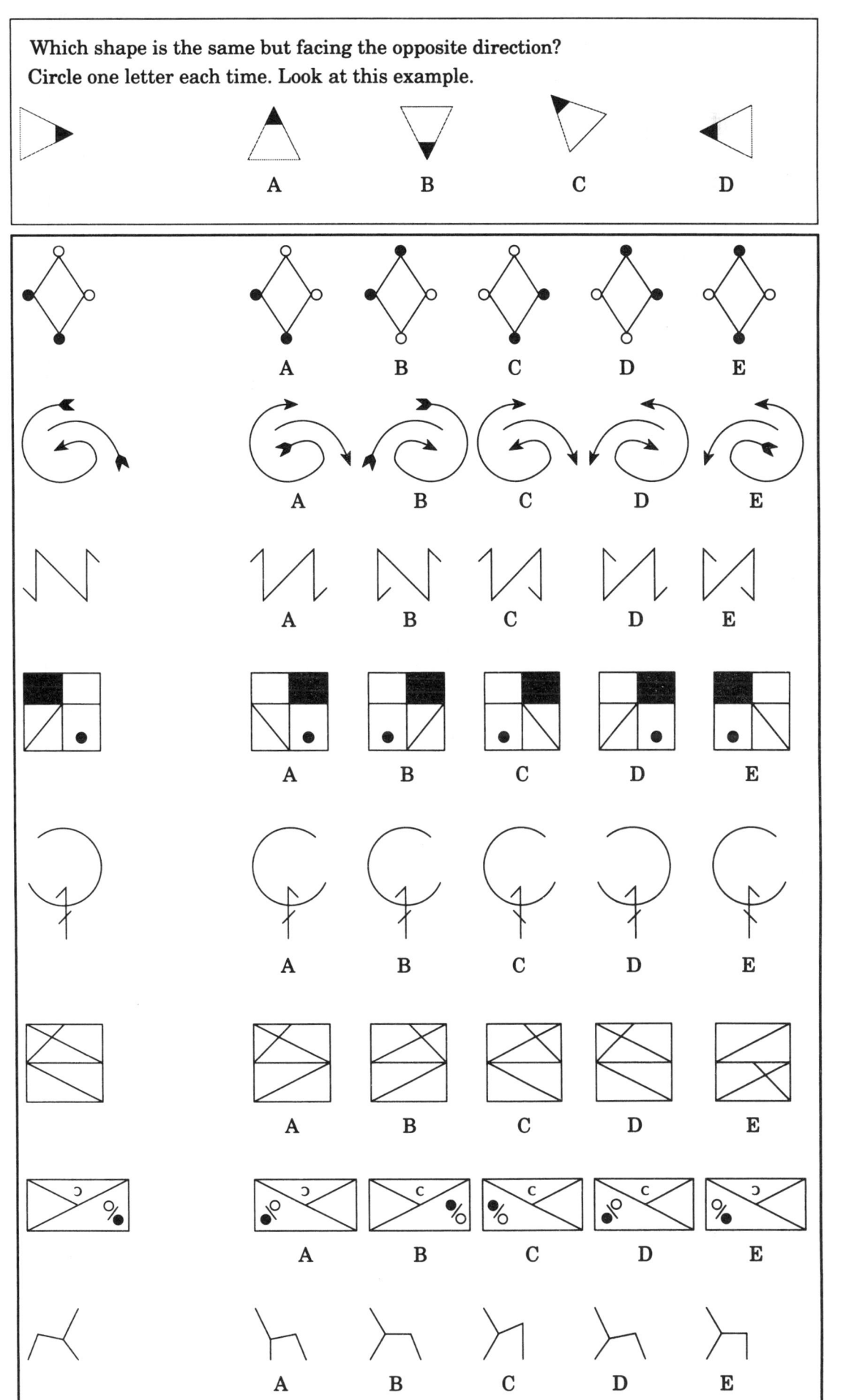

Which shape is different from the other four? Circle one letter each time.

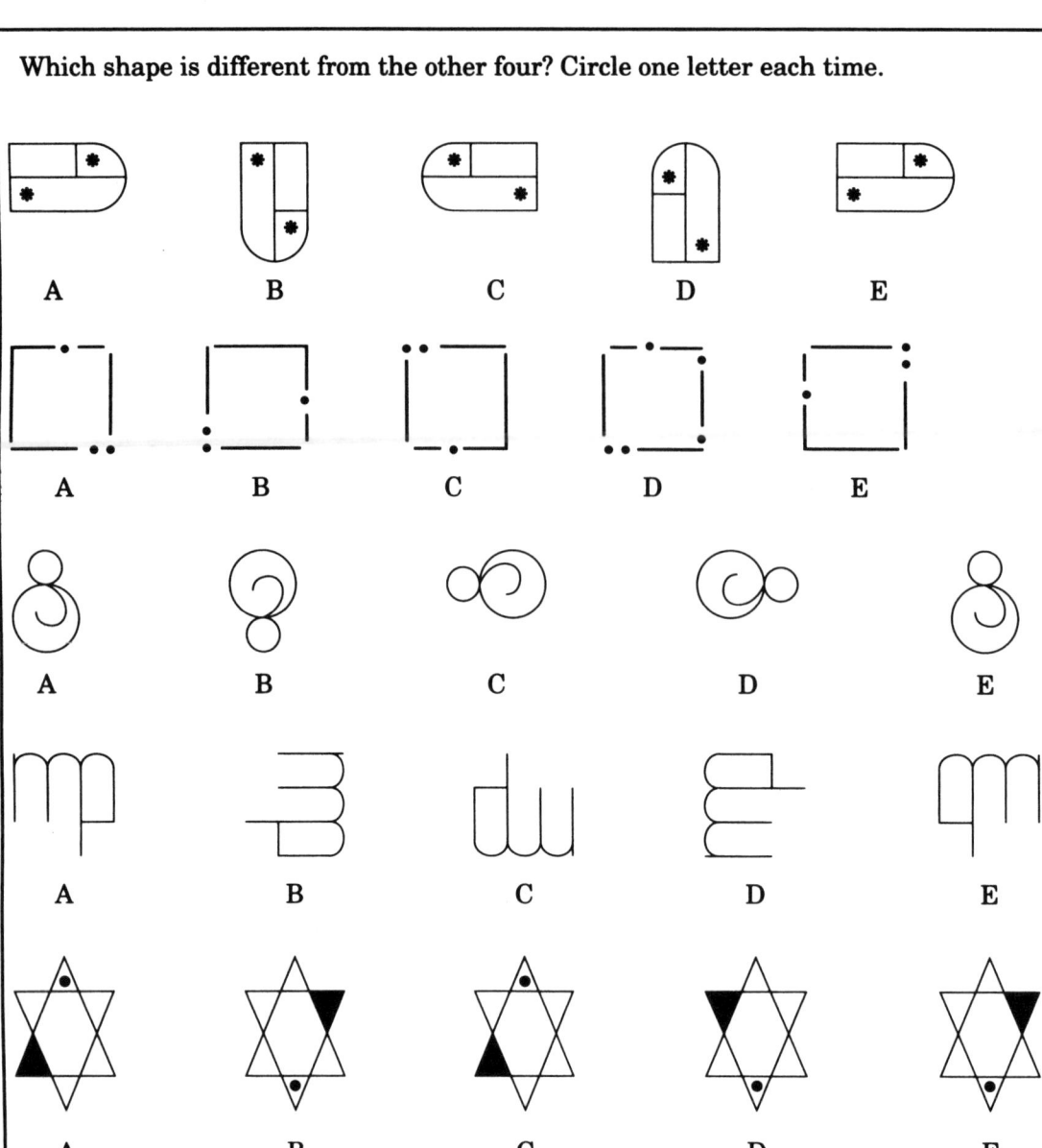

There are **two similar** shapes on the **left.**
Which **shape** on the **right** is **similar** to the **two shapes on the left?**
Circle the correct letter.

35.

A B C D E

36.

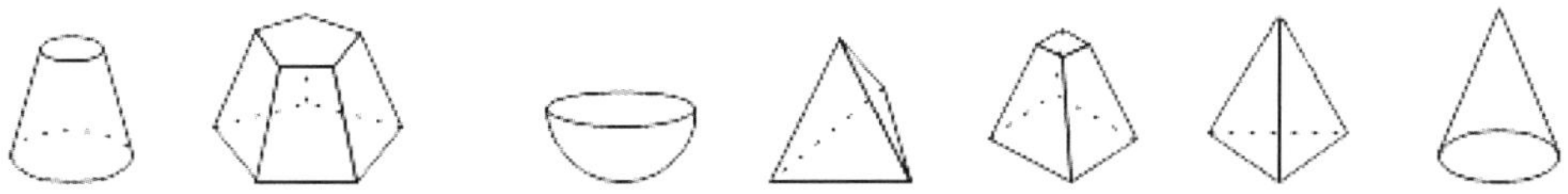

A B C D E

37.

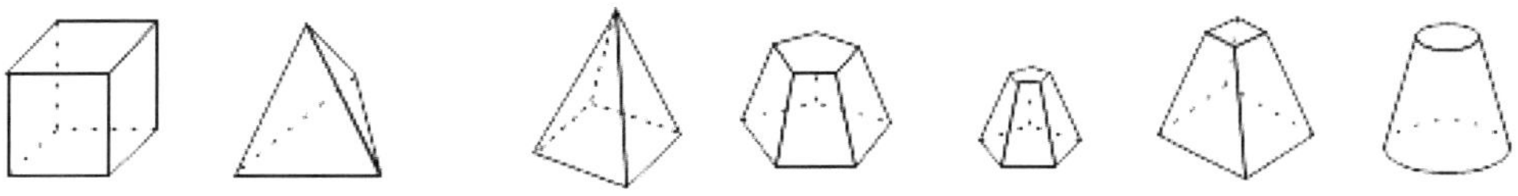

A B C D E

38.

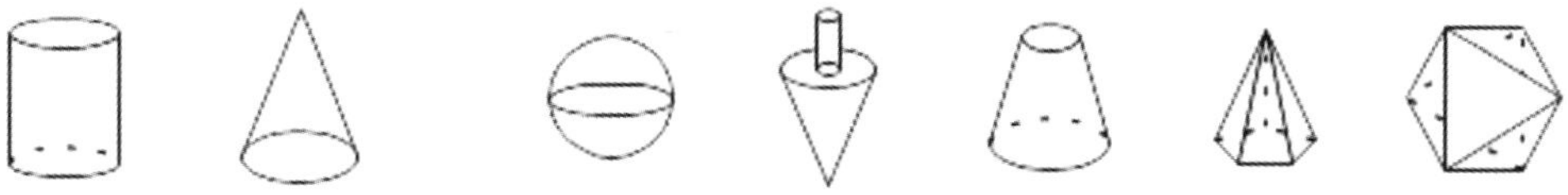

A B C D E

39.

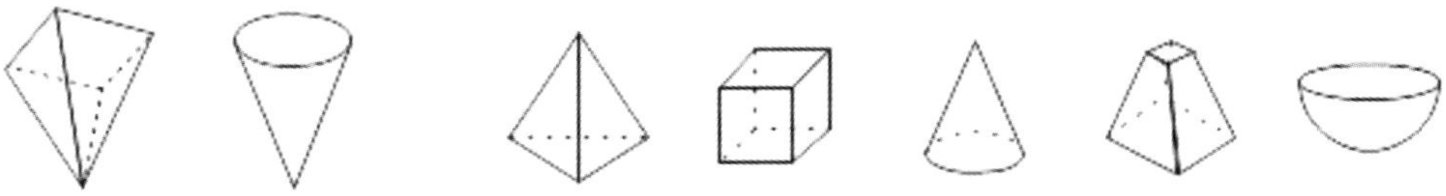

A B C D E

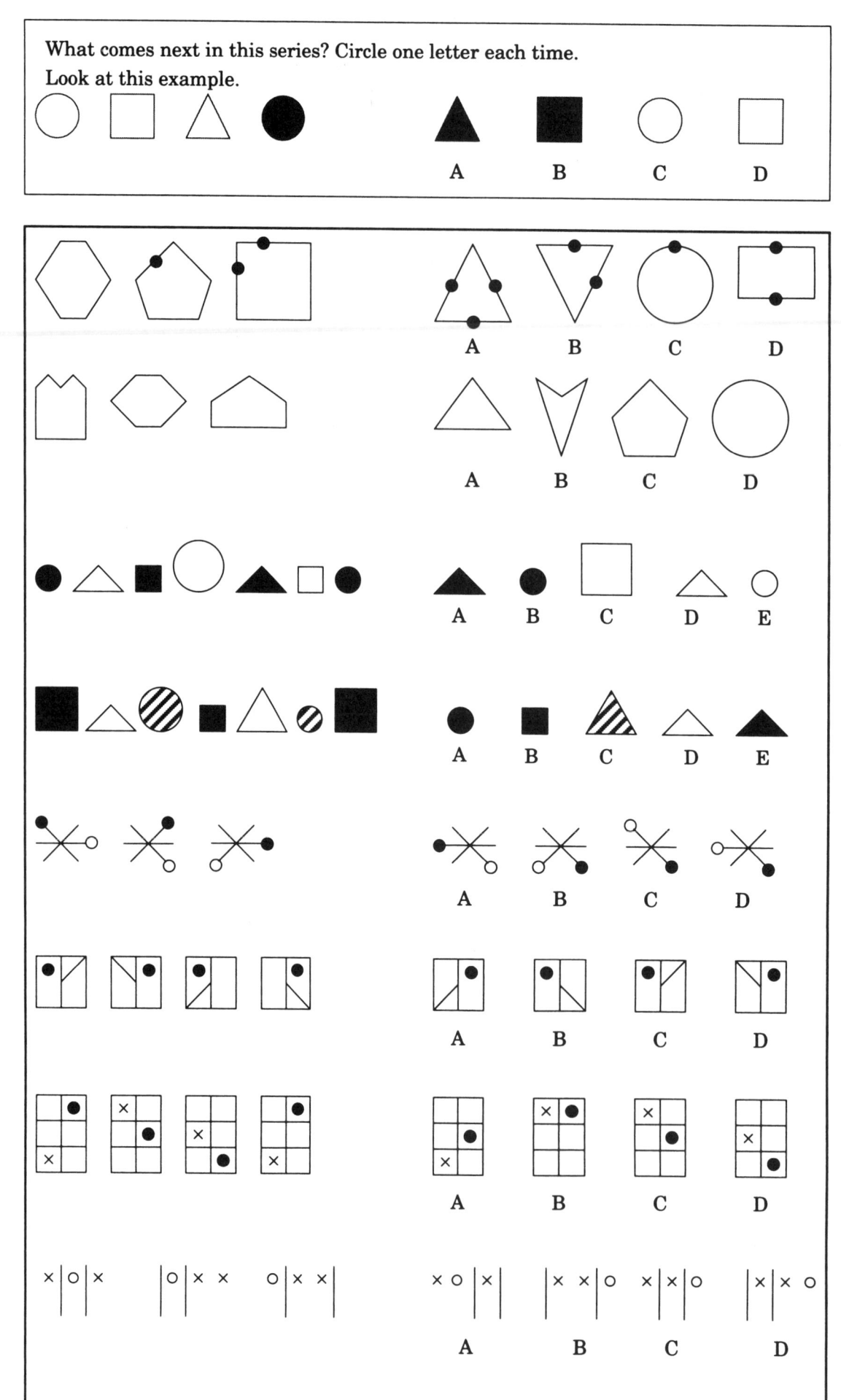

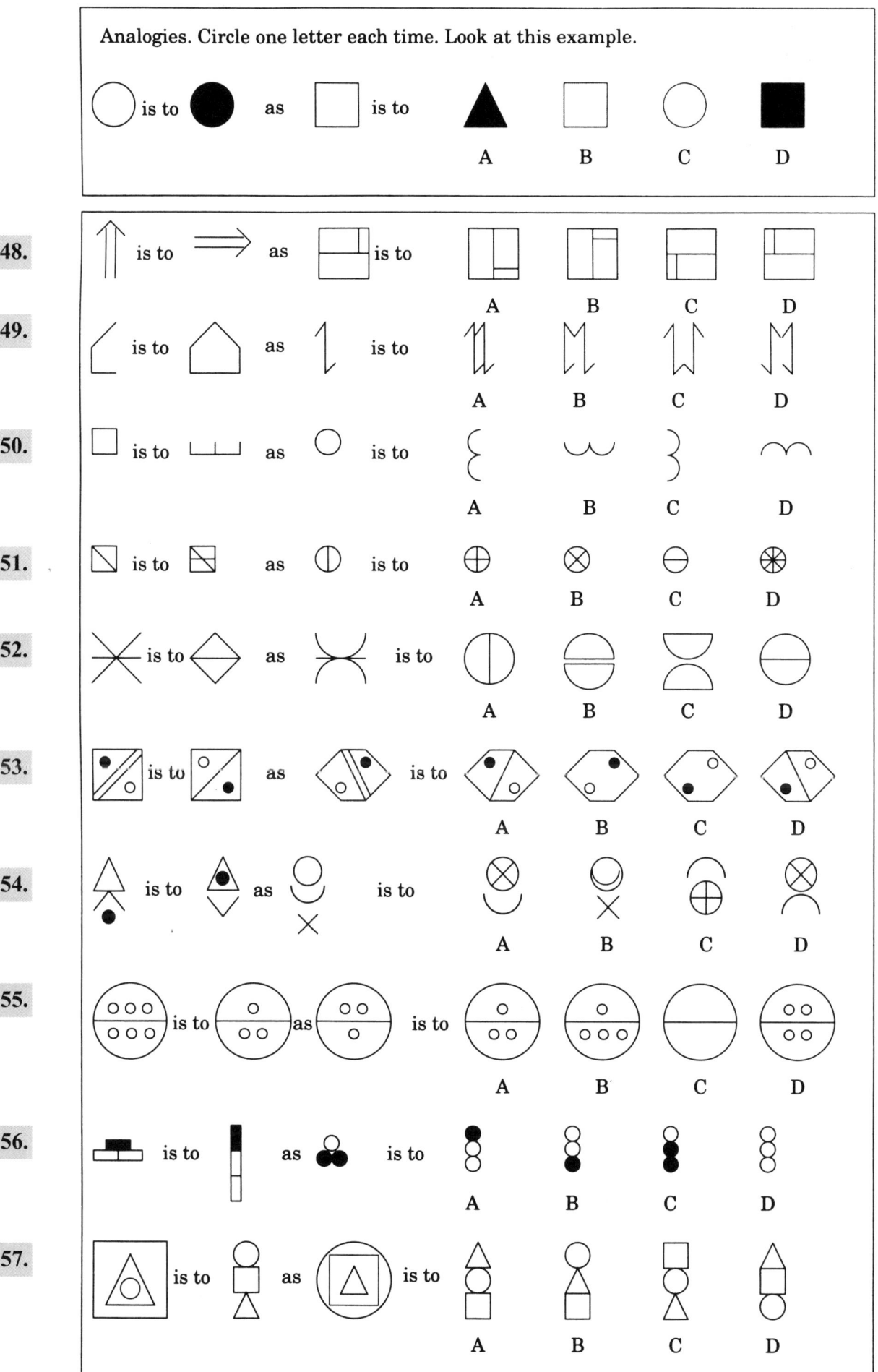

In these questions the two shapes are either added together or subtracted from each other. The shapes do not turn. Circle one answer. Look at this example.

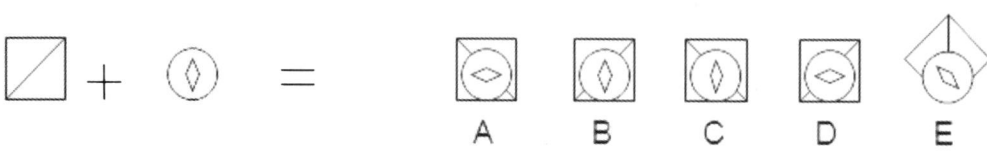

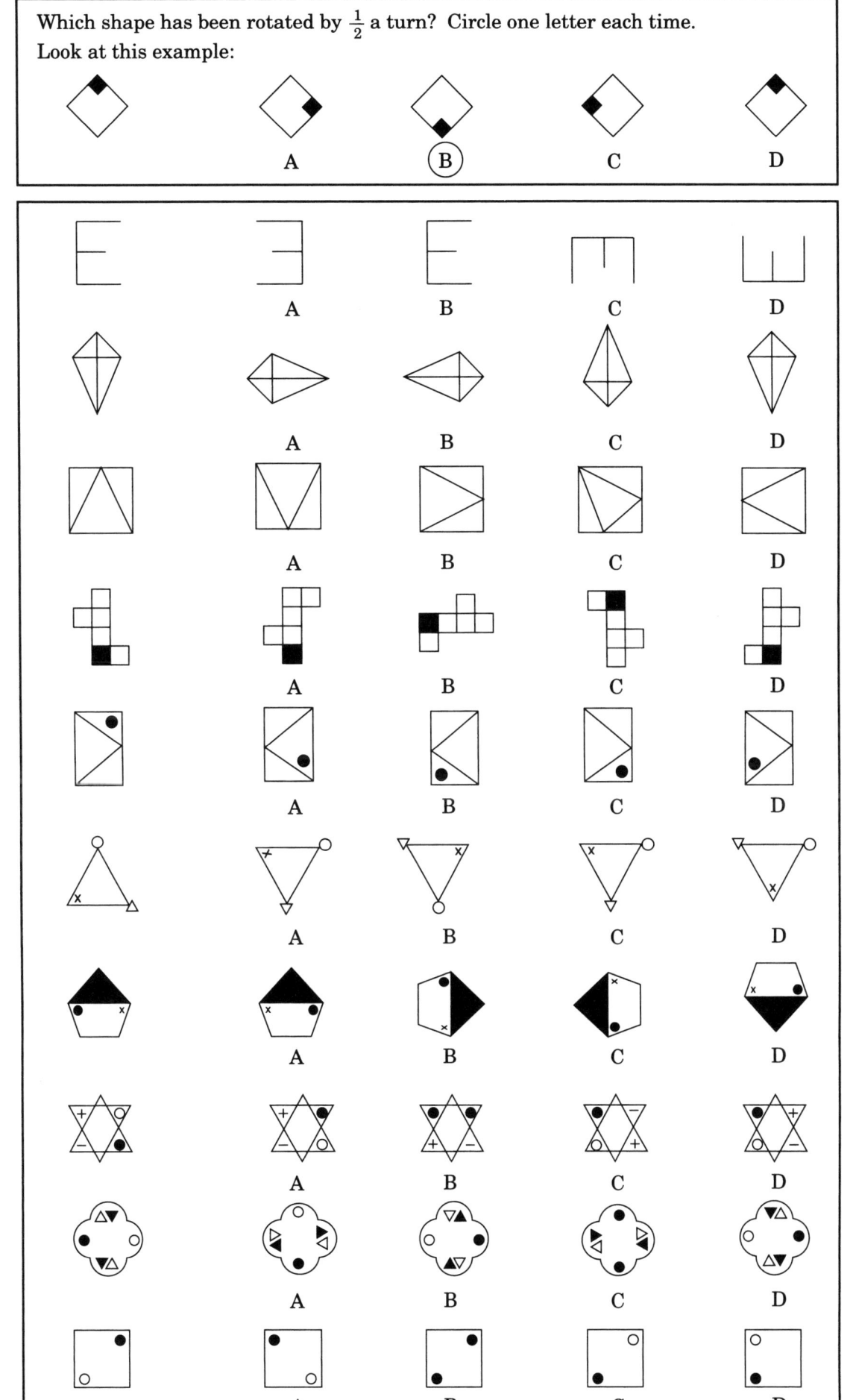

Answers to CEM Non-Verbal Reasoning Practice Test 5.

Question type					
Two The Same	1	C and E	Similar to Two on Left	39	A
	2	B and D	Series	40	A
	3	A and D		41	B
	4	A and E		42	D
	5	B and D		43	D
	6	B and D		44	D
Looking at 3D Shapes	7	A		45	C
	8	E		46	C
	9	A		47	B
	10	C	Analogies	48	A
	11	D		49	C
Odd One Out of Six	12	E		50	B
	13	E		51	A
	14	B		52	D
	15	C		53	D
	16	D		54	D
	17	D		55	C
	18	F		56	C
	19	D		57	A
	20	E	Adding and Substracting Shapes	58	C
	21	C		59	D
Reflections	22	C		60	A
	23	B		61	C
	24	A		62	D
	25	C		63	B
	26	E		64	D
	27	B		65	B
	28	D	Rotated by ½ a turn	66	A
	29	D		67	C
Four Similar Shapes and Fifth Different	30	C		68	A
	31	D		69	C
	32	B		70	B
	33	E		71	B
	34	D		72	D
Similar to Two on Left	35	D		73	C
	36	C		74	B
	37	A		75	C
	38	C			

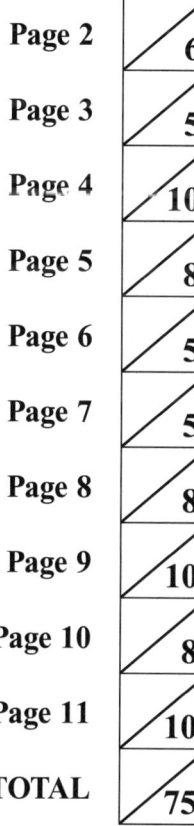

Page 2	6
Page 3	5
Page 4	10
Page 5	8
Page 6	5
Page 7	5
Page 8	8
Page 9	10
Page 10	8
Page 11	10
TOTAL	75

Web: - www.learningtogether.co.uk

Online 11+ platform: - www.onlineelevenplusexams.co.uk